THE CANDLE OF VISION

"THIS BOOK is one of the most important records of the mystic life ever written," says Leslie Shepard in the introduction to *The Candle of Vision*. The author, George William Russell, who first wrote anonymously under the initials AE but whose special genius could not long remain unacknowledged, was one of the leading figures in the Irish Literary Renaissance of the late nineteenth and early twentieth centuries. Yale University in this country honored him with the degree of Litt.D. He was closely associated with such outstanding poets and writers as W. B. Yeats, Charles Johnston, John Eglinton, and Charles Weekes in pursuing the study of mysticism.

The tendency to regard the mystic as a person far removed from everyday life is misleading in the case of George William Russell; he was deeply dedicated to the welfare of Ireland, his native country, was active in political movements, a leading thinker on rural cooperatives, and was frequently consulted on rural policy by the United States Department of Agriculture. Some of his writings were on subjects related to these activities. *The Candle of Vision,* for which he retained his pen name AE, is the distillation of the mystical insight which gave his own life meaning and purpose. "It is not a book for everybody," said one critic, "yet I wish everybody might read it."

TO

JAMES STEPHENS
BEST OF COMPANIONS

THE
Candle of Vision

by

AE
(George William Russell)

"The spirit of man is the candle of the Lord."—PROVERBS

"When his candle shined upon my head and by his light
I walked through darkness."—JOB

Introduction by Leslie Shepard

A QUEST BOOK
Published under a grant from the Kern Foundation

THE THEOSOPHICAL PUBLISHING HOUSE
Wheaton, Ill., U.S.A.
Madras, India / London, England

© 1965 by University Books, Inc.

First Quest Edition published by the
Theosophical Publishing House, Wheaton, Illinois,
a department of The Theosophical Society in America, 1974

Russell, George William, 1867-1935.
  The candle of vision.

  (A Quest book)
  Autobiographical.
  "A bibliography of 'AE' ": p.
  1. Russell, George William, 1867-1935.
I. Title.
PR6035.U7Z52 1974   291.4'2   73-17195
ISBN 0-8356-0445-4

INTRODUCTION

THIS BOOK is one of the most important records of the mystic life ever written.

That may seem very high praise for a modest volume, measured against the profundities of the Neoplatonists, Meister Eckhart, Jan van Ruysbroeck and many other august names, but the vision of the mystic is the same in all ages. The essential value of the present work is that it belongs to a period so relatively modern that it is easy for us to make contact with the book and the writer.

There is a tendency to regard the mystic as a superior and exalted person, far removed from the trivial and often absurd paraphernalia of everyday life, a remote person in a remote time and place, absorbed in communion with a higher world. We do not associate such rare individuals with the prosaic and materialistic twentieth century. Yet nothing could be more misleading, nor better contrived to falsify the true meaning of mysticism and the very real need for mystic insight in the lives of all of us.

The true mystic lives in two worlds. For him, the world of the spiritual life has as much reality as the material world of everyday affairs, and it is his task to integrate both worlds by his life and thought.

GEORGE WILLIAM RUSSELL, who wrote under the pen-name of "AE," is a supreme example of the true mystic.

This man was the key figure in a great Irish literary renaissance. He received an honorary degree of Litt.D. from Yale University, was consulted on rural policy by the U. S. Department of Agriculture. The President of the Irish Republic attended his funeral in Dublin.

Russell also made a profound impression on the brilliant writer A. R. Orage, famous for his association with another modern mystic — G. I. Gurdjieff.

Yet Russell's major inspiration came while he was a young clerk in a drapery shop in Dublin, studying theosophy in his spare time, and from this period also dates much of his important creative work, published anonymously under the initials "AE." The present book was written while he was editing a modest Dublin journal called *The Irish Homestead*, dedicated to agricultural reforms. Russell had no desire for fame, and if the secret of the enigmatic initials "AE" had not been revealed early in his career it is doubtful whether he would have laid personal claim to his most valued writings.

In the light of Russell's remarkable influence, it is surprising to find that his literary testament is a slim one. There are collections of poems, essays, pamphlets and books on political affairs and rural society. Most of these books are small in size. When one reads the appraisals of other writers like Orage, one gets the impression that there ought to be one large imposing work by Russell, but he was not a voluminous writer. All his books stem from a vision reflected unevenly throughout his poetry and prose. He said what he had to say without an imposing apparatus, and his inspiration could be condensed to a powerful phrase, a vivid image. In his strange mystical paintings his vision was freer and more direct; his poems might often be descriptions of paintings in their powerful visionary forms and vivid colours.

Of all his writings, the present book, which is concerned with mystic vision, is the most significant. In a detailed appreciation of this work, Orage wrote: "Rarely and more rarely does any artist or poet interest himself in the processes of his mental and spiritual life.... Only readers who can recall some experiences similar to those described by 'AE' will find themselves able to accept the work for what it is — a statement of uncommon fact; and only those who have developed their intuition to some degree will be able to appreciate the spirit of truth in which *The Candle of Vision* is written."

The high opinion of Orage is understandable, as his own career had interesting affinity with that of Russell.

Both were writers and editors. The literary vision of Orage
was affirmed by the contact with Gurdjieff; in the case of
Russell the influence was that of theosophy. But it must be
stressed that Russell was never a doctrinaire theosophist
and had no illusions about some of the shortcomings of the
movement. It was a catalyst that enhanced his own consciousness and brought about a true spiritual awakening.

Without an understanding of his mystic vision, the
facts of his career are only the bare bones of a life.

He was born 10 April 1867 in Lurgan, County Armagh,
Northern Ireland, where he attended the local Primitive
Methodist chapel, hardly a setting for a mystic. When he
was ten years old, the family moved to Dublin, where he
was educated at the Rathmines School. He discovered a
natural talent for painting, and from about the age of 13
attended the Metropolitan School of Art in Dublin. Here,
presently, he met William Butler Yeats, through whom he
was introduced to Theosophy. A Dublin Lodge of the
Theosophical Society was formed in 1886, with the en-
thusiastic support of Russell, Yeats, Charles Johnson, John
Eglinton, Charles Weekes and other leading intellectuals,
artists and writers. (The story of W. B. Yeats, his own
connection with mysticism, magic and yoga, and his part
in the Irish literary renaissance calls for separate study.)

About the time of his initiation to Theosophy, Russell
was obliged to earn a living by working as a clerk in a
brewery, later in a warehouse. From 1890 for several years
he served quietly as a clerk in Pim's drapery shop in
Dublin. During this period he wrote articles and poems
which were published in *The Irish Theosophist*. At the
drapery shop he was considered "wild-looking, but very
businesslike."

One day, in the same way that grace fell upon Jacob
Boehme, the shoemaker of Goerlitz, a strange spiritual
awakening had come to the young clerk in Dublin.

As Russell writes in *The Candle of Vision*: "I was
aged about sixteen or seventeen years, when I, the slackest
and least ideal of boys . . . became aware of a mysterious
life quickening within my life. . . . I began to be astonished

with myself, for, walking along country roads, intense and passionate imaginations of another world, of an interior nature, began to overpower me." The sweeping range of theosophical speculation, the treasures of ancient literature which it disclosed, dazzled his mind, shocked him into a heightened consciousness in which ancestral memories crowded with the titanic figures of Celtic myth. He painted with an uncanny skill these Blake-like visions which were, for him, tangible realities.

In one of these intense visionary paintings he tried to picture "the apparition in the Divine Mind of the idea of the Heavenly Man," and, as he puts it, something whispered to him "Call it the Birth of Aeon." It was only some time later, while visiting the Dublin National Library, that he saw with a shock the word "Aeon" in a book lying casually open on the counter; afterwards he read for the first time of the Gnostics, their visions of spiritual emanation and the angelic Aeons.

He signed one of his articles "AEON," and a proofreader who could not decipher the word rendered this "AE-?." Russell accepted the initials and thereafter never wrote under his own name.

In 1894, through the interest of Yeats and Charles Weekes, a first small volume of poems by Russell was published: *Homeward: Songs by the Way.* This book made a great impression and other slim volumes followed. About this time Sir Horace Plunkett formed the Irish Agricultural Organization Society, dedicated to establishing cooperatives among the farmers. In 1897 Russell became an organizer for this society, preaching the gospel of cooperation throughout rural Ireland. In 1898, when the theosophists objected to him combining Theosophy with rural economics, he left them, but remained a theosophist at heart. In the same year he married Violet North; they had two sons, one of whom became an American citizen.

From 1905 onwards, Russell was Editor of the journal *The Irish Homestead* and its successor *The Irish Statesman;* through the years he wrote articles, pamphlets, and poems. He wrote about fifteen columns of journalism every

week, spending five and a half days at work and the week-
ends in occasional visits to the quiet countryside and in
reading and painting.

In a letter to James M. Pryse he wrote in wry com-
plaint: "Painting is the only thing I have any real delight
in doing. Nature intended me to be a painter.... I went
into an office, and wrote poetry. Then because I wrote good
poetry I was taken from the office and sent out over the
country to organize farmers. When I wrote two or three
articles about farmers and their lives I was taken from
organising and put on to editing an agricultural paper.
When I had learned to do this I was dragged into politics,
and now I edit a weekly review dealing with politics, literature and economics."

In fact, he voluntarily renounced his remarkable talent
in painting so far as earning a living was concerned, although there is little doubt that he might have become a
distinguished artist. In one of his letters he wrote: "I do
not think I will ever try to get either literary or artistic
fame; art and literature do not interest me now, only one
thing interests me and that is life or truth. I want to become rather than to know." This is the true aim of the
mystic, expressed perhaps in its clearest form in the ancient
Indian scripture *Bhagavada Gita*, a work which had greatly
impressed Russell.

After this mystical affirmation his own plans had little
effect on his future. Once a man has seen reality with his
inner eye and acknowledged its truth, he can no longer
order his destiny. Against his own desire Russell became
famous, and even helped many others to become famous.
He was caught up in the currents of his time but in his
central being remained aloof.

In the troubled years of Ireland he did not hesitate
to express his opinions, although with tact and wisdom.
During the great Dublin Labor disputes in 1913 he travelled to London and addressed a great protest meeting at
the Albert Hall, in company with George Bernard Shaw.
Forty thousand people listened.

In 1919 he wrote "I am tied for my sins to movements, and do my best in them, but I am remote from them while I am in them."

He made several trips to the United States, where he was warmly received, lecturing mostly on agricultural affairs. He had a great affection for America, its vastness and the hospitality of its people, but he was happiest, as he once wrote to poet Vachel Lindsay, staying in a remote mountainy district in Donegal, Ireland — "I eat griddle bread, drink buttermilk, sit by a turf fire, and walk over hills and sands. . . ."

After the death of his wife in 1932, he sold his house and lived part of the time in England. He had never been a rich man and much of his life was spent on a fixed income of less than $500 a year. In 1934 he wrote to Van Wyck Brooks: "We are all poor in Ireland. . . . So many artists want a motor-car, a house, to give parties, etc., that they sell their genius for cash. They should all take the vow of poverty that is an inside vow."

He also wrote: ". . . I live now very economically as my fixed income is about £100 a year, and am I unhappy? Good God, no . . . I lived with an income varying from thirty to sixty pounds and was magnificently happy. Yeats had long years of poverty and never sold his talent. Stephens was living on one pound a week when he wrote *The Charwoman's Daughter* and *The Crock of Gold* and the early poems. Stephen MacKenna, the translator of Plotinus, the greatest piece of prose written in our time, lived at the end of his life on two pounds a week . . ."

After a sudden illness on an American tour, he returned to England, where he died, at Bournemouth 17 July 1935, at the age of 68. The Preface to his very first book of poems, *Homewards*, is a fitting epitaph:

> "I moved among men and places, and in living I learned the truth at last. I know that I am a spirit, and that I went forth in old time from the Self-ancestral to labours yet unaccomplished; but filled ever and again with home-sickness I made these songs by the way."

The Candle of Vision is his most self-revelatory book, the autobiography of a mystic. He explains in his preface:

"I have tried according to my capacity to report about the divine order and to discriminate between that which was self-begotten fantasy and that which came from a higher sphere." This fine discrimination is particularly noticeable when he moves from visions and speculations to direct intuition.

He had practised meditation and developed unusual gifts. He once said: "I have discovered that consciousness can exist outside the body, that we can sometimes see people who are far away from us, that we can even speak to them when they are hundreds of miles distant: I have been spoken to myself in this way. I know by experience that disembodied beings may act upon us profoundly. I am convinced that I remember past lives, and I have spoken with friends who remembered them equally. . . . I have also seen elemental beings, and people with me have seen them at the same time."

Here are twenty chapters, each self-contained, dealing with an important phase of higher consciousness, but all linked by the visionary spirit which runs all through this work, the same inspired knowledge that flooded the dingy office where Russell worked as a clerk and transformed the drab everyday scene with meaning and purpose.

In this wonderful book Russell writes in the jewelled phrases of a poet on mystic consciousness, cosmic intuition and imaginative vision, as a true knowledge to be shared with other people. He writes as he lived, in utter sincerity.

This book is an essential key, not only to Russell, but also to the mystic life itself, which is the inheritance of everyone. Few critics understood this better than A. R. Orage, who wrote that it "is not a book for everybody, yet I wish that everybody might read it."

LESLIE SHEPARD

12 Moatlands House
Cromer Street
London, W.C.1.
England

March 1965

A Bibliography of "AE"

POETRY:

Homeward: Songs by the Way 1894
The Earth Breath and Other Poems 1897
The Divine Vision and Other Poems 1903
The Nuts of Knowledge 1903
By Still Waters 1906
Collected Poems 1913
Gods of War and Other Poems 1915
Voices of the Stones 1925
Midsummer Eve 1928
Dark Weeping 1929
Enchantment and Other Poems 1930
Vale and Other Poems 1931
The House of the Titans and Other Poems 1934
Selected Poems 1935

PROSE:

The Mask of Apollo and Other Stories 1904
Some Irish Essays 1906
Deirdre (play) 1907
The Hero in Man 1909
The Renewal of Youth 1911
Co-operation and Nationality 1912
Imaginations and Reveries 1915
The National Being 1916
Thoughts on Irish Polity 1917
The Candle of Vision 1918
The Interpreters 1920
Song and Its Fountains 1932
The Avatars: A Futurist Fantasy 1933
*Some Passages from the Letters of AE to
W. B. Yeats* 1936
The Living Torch. Selected Prose (Edited, with an Introductory Essay, by Monk Gibbon) 1937

Biographies

Boyd, Ernest A. *Ireland's Literary Renaissance* 1923
Clyde, William M. *A.E.* 1935
Eglinton, John. (W. K. Magee). *A Memoir of AE* 1937
Figgis, Darrell. *AE—George W. Russell; A Study of
a man and a Nation* 1916
Orage, A. R. *Readers and Writers, 1917-1921*
(includes important chapter on *AE* and
The Candle of Vision) 1922

PREFACE

WHEN I am in my room looking upon the walls I have painted I see there reflections of the personal life, but when I look through the windows I see a living nature and land-scapes not painted by hands. So, too, when I meditate I feel in the images and thoughts which throng about me the reflections of personality, but there are also windows in the soul through which can be seen images created not by human but by the divine imagination. I have tried according to my capacity to report about the divine order and to discriminate between that which was self-begotten fantasy and that which came from a higher sphere. These retrospects and meditations are the efforts of an artist and poet to relate his own vision to the vision of the seers and writers of the sacred books, and to discover what element of truth lay in those imaginations.

A. E.

CONTENTS

RETROSPECT

I HAD travelled all day and was tired, but I could not rest by the hearth in the cottage on the hill. My heart was beating with too great an excitement. After my year in the city I felt like a child who wickedly stays from home through a long day, and who returns frightened and penitent at nightfall, wondering whether it will be received with forgiveness by its mother. Would the Mother of us all receive me again as one of her children? Would the winds with wandering voices be as before the evangelists of her love? Or would I feel like an outcast amid the mountains, the dark valleys and the shining lakes? I knew if benediction came how it would come. I would sit among the rocks with shut eyes, waiting humbly as one waits in the ante-chambers of the mighty, and if the invisible ones chose me as companion they would begin with a soft breathing of their intimacies, creeping on me with shadowy affection like children who steal nigh to the bowed head and suddenly whisper fondness in the ear before it has even heard a footfall. So I stole out of the cottage and over the dark ridges to the place of rocks, and sat down, and let the coolness of the night chill and still the fiery dust in the brain. I waited trembling for the faintest touch, the shyest breathing of the Everlasting within my soul, the sign of reception and forgiveness. I knew it would come. I could not so desire what was not my own, and what is our own we cannot lose. Desire is hidden identity. The darkness drew me heavenward. From the hill the plains beneath slipped away grown vast and vague, remote and still. I seemed alone with immensity, and there came at last that melting of the divine darkness into the life within me for which I prayed. Yes, I still belonged, however humbly, to the heavenly household. I was not outcast. Still, though by a thread fine as that by which a spider hangs from the rafters, my being was suspended from the habitations of eternity. I longed to throw my arms about the hills, to meet with kisses the lips of the seraph wind. I felt the gaiety of childhood springing up through weariness and age, for to come into contact with that which is eternally young is to have that childhood of the spirit it must attain ere it can be moulded by the Magician of the Beautiful and enter the House of Many Mansions.

I had not always this intimacy with nature. I never felt a light in childhood which faded in manhood into the common light of day, nor do I believe that childhood is any nearer than age to this being. If it were so what would the spirit have to hope for after youth was gone? I was not conscious in my boyhood of any heaven lying about me. I lived in the city, and the hills from which aid was to come to me were only a far flush of blue on the horizon. Yet I was drawn to them, and as years passed and legs grew longer I came nearer and nearer until at last one day I found myself on the green hillside. I came to play with other boys, but years were yet to pass before the familiar places grew strange once more and the mountains dense with fiery forms and awful as Sinai.

While the child is still in its mother's arms it is nourished by her, yet it does not know it is a mother which feeds it. It knows later in whose bosom it has lain. As the mother nourishes the body so the Mighty

Mother nourishes the soul. Yet there are but few who pay reverence where reverence is due, and that is because this benign deity is like a mother who indulges the fancies of her children. With some she imparts life to their own thoughts. Others she endows with the vision of her own heart. Even of these last some love in silence, being afraid to speak of the majesty which smiled on them, and others deceived think with pride : " This vision is my own."

I was like these last for a long time. I was aged about sixteen or seventeen years, when I, the slackest and least ideal of boys, with my life already made dark by those desires of body and heart with which we so soon learn to taint our youth, became aware of a mysterious life quickening within my life. Looking back I know not of anything in friendship, anything I had read, to call this forth. It was, I thought, self-begotten. I began to be astonished with myself, for, walking along country roads, intense and passionate imaginations of another world, of an interior nature began to overpower me. They were like strangers who suddenly enter a house, who brush aside the doorkeeper, and who will not be denied. Soon I knew

they were the rightful owners and heirs of
the house of the body, and the doorkeeper
was only one who was for a time in charge,
who had neglected his duty, and who had
pretended to ownership. The boy who
existed before was an alien. He hid himself
when the pilgrim of eternity took up his abode
in the dwelling. Yet, whenever the true
owner was absent, the sly creature reappeared
and boasted himself as master once more.

That being from a distant country who
took possession of the house began to speak
in a language difficult to translate. I was
tormented by limitations of understanding.
Somewhere about me I knew there were
comrades who were speaking to me, but I
could not know what they said. As I walked
in the evening down the lanes scented by
the honeysuckle my senses were expectant of
some unveiling about to take place, I felt that
beings were looking in upon me out of the
true home of man. They seemed to be saying
to each other of us, " Soon they will awaken ;
soon they will come to us again," and for a
moment I almost seemed to mix with their
eternity. The tinted air glowed before me
with intelligible significance like a face, a voice.
The visible world became like a tapestry

blown and stirred by winds behind it.   If it
would but raise for an instant I knew I would
be in Paradise.   Every form on that tapestry
appeared to be the work of gods.   Every
flower was a word, a thought.   The grass was
speech ; the trees were speech ; the waters
were speech ; the winds were speech.   They
were the Army of the Voice marching on to
conquest and dominion over the spirit ; and
I listened with my whole being, and then these
apparitions would fade away and I would be
the mean and miserable boy once more.   So
might one have felt who had been servant of
the prophet, and had seen him go up in the
fiery chariot, and the world had no more light
or certitude in it with that passing.   I knew
these visitations for what they were and named
them truly in my fantasy, for writing then in
the first verses of mine which still seem to
me to be poetry, I said of the earth that we
and all things were her dreams :

> She is rapt in dreams divine.
> As her clouds of beauty pass
> On our glowing hearts they shine,
> Mirrored there as in a glass.
>
> Earth, whose dreams are we and they,
> With her deep heart's gladness fills
> All our human lips can say
> Or the dawn-fired singer trills.

Yet such is human nature that I still felt vanity as if this vision was mine, and I acted like one who comes across the treasure-house of a king, and spends the treasure as if it were his own. We may indeed have a personal wisdom, but spiritual vision is not to speak of as ours any more than we can say at the rising of the sun : "This glory is mine." By the sudden uprising of such vanities in the midst of vision I was often outcast, and found myself in an instant like those warriors of Irish legend, who had come upon a lordly house and feasted there and slept, and when they woke they were on the barren hillside, and the Faed Fia was drawn about that lordly house. Yet though the imagination apprehended truly that this beauty was not mine, and hailed it by its heavenly name, for some years my heart was proud, for as the beauty sank into memory it seemed to become a personal possession, and I said " I imagined this " when I should humbly have said, " The curtain was a little lifted that I might see." But the day was to come when I could not deny the Mighty Mother the reverence due, when I was indeed to know by what being I had been nourished, and to be made sweet and mad as a lover with the consciousness of her intermingling spirit.

The sages of old found that at the close of intense meditation their being was drawn into union with that which they contemplated. All desire tends to bring about unity with the object adored, and this is no less true of spiritual and elemental than of bodily desire ; and I, with my imagination more and more drawn to adore an ideal nature, was tending to that vital contact in which what at first was apprehended in fantasy would become the most real of all things. When that certitude came I felt as Dante might have felt after conceiving of Beatrice close at his side and in the Happy World, if, after believing it a dream, half hoping that it might here-after be a reality, that beloved face before his imagination grew suddenly intense, vivid and splendidly shining, and he knew beyond all doubt that her spirit was truly in that form, and had descended to dwell in it, and would be with him for evermore. So did I feel one warm summer day lying idly on the hillside, not then thinking of anything but the sunlight, and how sweet it was to drowse there, when, suddenly, I felt a fiery heart throb, and knew it was personal and intimate, and started with every sense dilated and intent, and turned inwards, and I heard first a music as of bells going away, away into that wondrous underland whither, as legend relates, the Danaan gods withdrew ; and then the heart of the hills was opened to me, and I knew there was no hill for those who were there, and they were unconscious of the ponderous mountain piled above the palaces of light, and the winds were sparkling and diamond clear, yet full of colour as an opal, as they glittered through the valley, and I knew the Golden Age was all about me, and it was we who had been blind to it but that it had never passed away from the world.

THE EARTH BREATH

AFTER that awakening earth began more and more to bewitch me, and to lure me to her heart with honied entreaty. I could not escape from it even in that busy office where I sat during week-days with little heaps of paper mounting up before me moment by frenzied moment. An interval of inactivity and I would be aware of that sweet eternal presence overshadowing me. I was an exile from living nature but she yet visited me. Her ambassadors were visions that made me part of themselves. Through the hot foetid air of the gaslit room I could see the feverish faces, the quick people flitting about, and hear the voices; and then room, faces and voices would be gone, and I would be living in the Mother's being in some pure, remote, elemental region of hers. Instead of the dingy office there would be a sky of rarest amethyst; a snow - cold bloom of

cloud ; high up in the divine wilderness,
solitary, a star ; all rapt, breathless and still ;
rapt the seraph princes of wind and wave
and fire, for it was the hour when the King,
an invisible presence, moved through His
dominions and Nature knew and was hushed
at the presence of her Lord.   Once, suddenly,
I found myself on some remote plain or steppe,
and heard unearthly chimes pealing passion-
ately from I know not what far steeples.
The earth-breath streamed from the furrows
to the glowing heavens.   Overhead the birds
flew round and round crying their incomprehensible cries, as if they were maddened, and
knew not where to nestle, and had dreams
of some more enraptured rest in a diviner
home.   I could see a ploughman lifting himself from his obscure toil and stand with lit
eyes as if he too had been fire-smitten and
was caught into heaven as I was, and knew
for that moment he was a god.   And then
I would lapse out of vision and ecstasy, and
hear the voices, and see again through the
quivering of the hot air the feverish faces,
and seem to myself to be cast out of the
spirit.   I could hardly bear after thinking of
these things, for I felt I was trapped in some
obscure hell.   You, too, trapped with me,

dear kindly people, who never said a harsh word to the forgetful boy. You, too, I knew, had your revelations. I remember one day how that clerk with wrinkled face, blinking eyes and grizzly beard, who never seemed, apart from his work, to have interests other than his pipe and paper, surprised me by telling me that the previous midnight he waked in his sleep, and some self of him was striding to and fro in the moonlight in an avenue mighty with gigantic images ; and that dream self he had surprised had seemed to himself unearthly in wisdom and power. What had he done to be so high in one sphere and so petty in another ? Others I could tell of, too, who had their moment of awe when the spirit made its ancient claim on them. But none were so happy or so unhappy as I was. I was happy at times because the divine world which had meant nothing to my childhood was becoming a reality to manhood : and I knew it was not a dream, for comrades in vision soon came to me, they who could see as I saw, and hear as I heard, and there were some who had gone deeper into that being than I have ever travelled. I was more miserable than my work-a-day companions, because the

very intensity of vision made the recoil more
unendurable.   It was an agony of darkness
and oblivion, wherein I seemed like those
who in nightmare are buried in caverns so
deep beneath the roots of the world that
there is no hope of escape, for the way out is
unknown, and the way to them is forgotten
by those who walk in light.   In those black
hours the universe, a gigantic presence,
seemed at war with me.   I was condemned,
I thought, to be this speck of minute life
because of some sin committed in remote
ages, I and those with me.   We were all lost
children of the stars.   Everything that suggested our high original being, a shaft of
glory from the far fire in the heavens spear-
ing the gloom of the office, the blue twilight
deepening through the panes until it was
rich with starry dust, the sunny clouds career
ing high over the city, these things would
stir pangs of painful remembrance and my
eyes would suddenly grow blind and wet.
Sometimes, too, I would rebel and plot in
my obscurity, and remember moments when
the will in me seemed to be a titanic power,
and my spirit would brood upon ways of
escape and ascent to its native regions, as
those fallen angels in Milton's tremendous

narrative rose up from torture, and conspired to tear the throne from Him.   And then all that would appear to me to be futile as a speck of dust trying to stay itself against the typhoon, and the last door would close upon me and leave me more hopeless than before.

THE SLAVE OF THE LAMP

BECAUSE I was a creature of many imaginings
and of rapid alternations of mood out of
all that there came to me assurance of a
truth, of all truths most inspiring to one in
despair in the Iron Age and lost amid the
undergrowths of being. I became aware of
a swift echo or response to my own moods
in circumstance which had seemed hitherto
immutable in its indifference. I found every
intense imagination, every new adventure of
the intellect endowed with magnetic power to
attract to it its own kin. Will and desire
were as the enchanter's wand of fable, and
they drew to themselves their own affinities.
Around a pure atom of crystal all the atoms
of the element in solution gather, and in like
manner one person after another emerged out
of the mass, betraying their close affinity to
my moods as they were engendered. I met
these people seemingly by accident along

country roads, or I entered into conversation with strangers and found they were intimates of the spirit. I could prophesy from the uprising of new moods in myself that I, without search, would soon meet people of a certain character, and so I met them. Even inanimate things were under the sway of these affinities. They yielded up to me what they had specially for my eyes. I have glanced in passing at a book left open by some one in a library, and the words first seen thrilled me, for they confirmed a knowledge lately attained in vision. At another time a book taken down idly from a shelf opened at a sentence quoted from a Upanishad, scriptures then to me unknown, and this sent my heart flying eastwards because it was the answer to a spiritual problem I had been brooding over an hour before. It was hardly a week after my first awakening that I began to meet those who were to be my lifelong comrades on the quest, and who were, like myself, in a. boyhood troubled by the spirit. I had just attempted to write in verse when I met a boy whose voice was soon to be the most beautiful voice in Irish literature. I sought none of these out because I had heard of them and surmised a kinship. The concurrence of our

personalities seemed mysterious and controlled
by some law of spiritual gravitation, like that
which in the chemistry of nature makes one
molecule fly to another.   I remember the
exultation with which I realised about life
that, as Heraclitus has said, it was in a flux,
and that in all its flowings there was meaning
and law ; that I could not lose what was my
own ; I need not seek, for what was my own
would come to me ; if any passed it was
because they were no longer mine.   One
buried in a dungeon for many years could
not have hailed sunshine, the sweet-smelling
earth, and the long hidden infinitude of the
skies more joyously than I the melting of that
which had seemed immutable.   It is those who
live and grow swiftly, and who continually com-
pare what is without with what is within, who
have this certainty.   Those who do not change
see no change and recognise no law.   He who
has followed even in secrecy many lights of the
spirit can see one by one the answering torches
gleam.   When I was made certain about this
I accepted what befell with resignation.   I
knew that all I met was part of myself and
that what I could not comprehend was related
by affinity to some yet unrealised forces in
my being.   We have within us the Lamp of

the World ; and Nature, the genie, is Slave of
the Lamp, and must fashion life about us as
we fashion it within ourselves.   What we are
alone has power.   We may give up the outward personal struggle and ambition, and if
we leave all to the Law all that is rightly ours
will be paid.   Man becomes truly the Super-
man when he has this proud consciousness.
No matter where he may be, in what seeming
obscurity, he is still the King, still master of
his fate, and circumstance reels about him or
is still as he, in the solitude of his spirit, is
mighty or is humble.   We are indeed most
miserable when we dream we have no power
over circumstance, and I account it the
highest wisdom to know this of the living
universe that there is no destiny in it other
than that we make for ourselves.   How the
spirit is kindled, how it feels its power, when,
outwardly quiet, it can see the coming and
going of life, as it dilates within itself or
is still !   Then do we move in miracle and
wonder.   Then does the universe appear to
us as it did to the Indian sage who said that
to him who was perfect in meditation all rivers
were sacred as the Ganges and all speech
was holy.

MEDITATION

THERE is no personal virtue in me other than this that I followed a path all may travel but on which few do journey. It is a path within ourselves where the feet first falter in shadow and darkness but which is later made gay by heavenly light. As one who has travelled a little on that way and who has had some far-off vision of the Many-Coloured Land, if I tell what I know, and how I came to see most clearly, I may give hope to those who would fain believe in that world the seers spake of, but who cannot understand the language written by those who had seen that beauty of old, or who may have thought the ancient scriptures but a record of extravagant desires. None need special gifts or genius. Gifts! There are no gifts. For all that is ours we have paid the price. There is nothing we aspire to for which we cannot barter some spiritual merchandise of our own. Genius!

There is no stinting of this by the Keeper of the Treasure House.   It is not bestowed but is won.   Yon man of heavy soul might if he willed play on the lyre of Apollo, that drunkard be god-intoxicated.   Powers are not bestowed by caprice on any.   The formulae the chemist illustrates, making   exposition   before   his students, are not more certainly verifiable than the formulae of that alchemy by which what is gross in us may be transmuted into ethereal fires.   Our religions make promises to be fulfilled beyond the grave because they have no knowledge now to be put to the test, but the ancients spake of a divine vision to be attained while we are yet in the body. The religion which does not cry out : " I am to-day verifiable as that water wets or that fire burns.   Test me that ye can become as gods." Mistrust it.   Its messengers are prophets of the darkness.   As we sink deeper into the Iron Age we are met by the mighty devils of state and empire lurking in the abyss, claiming the soul for their own, moulding it to their image, to be verily their own creature and not heaven's.   We need a power in ourselves that   can   confront   these   mighty   powers. Though I am blind I have had moments of sight.   Though I have sinned I have been on

the path. Though I am feeble I have seen
the way to power. I sought out ways to
make more securely my own those magical
lights that dawned and faded within me. I
wished to evoke them at will and be master
of my vision, and I was taught to do this
which is as old as human life. Day after
day, at times where none might interfere, and
where none through love or other cause were
allowed to interfere, I set myself to attain
mastery over the will. I would choose some
mental object, an abstraction of form, and
strive to hold my mind fixed on it in unwavering concentration, so that not for a
moment, not for an instant, would the concentration slacken. It is an exercise this, a
training for higher adventures of the soul.
It is no light labour. The ploughman's,
cleaving the furrows, is easier by far. Five
minutes of this effort will at first leave us
trembling as at the close of a laborious day.
It is then we realise how little of life has
been our own, and how much a response to
sensation, a drifting on the tide of desire.
The rumour of revolt, the spirit would
escape its thraldom, runs through the body.
Empires do not send legions so swiftly to
frustrate revolt as all that is mortal in us

hurries along nerve, artery, and every high-
way of the body to beset the soul. The
beautiful face of one we love, more alluring
than life, glows before us to enchant us from
our task. Old sins, enmities, vanities and
desires beleaguer and beseech us. If we do
not heed them then they change, they seem to
be with us, they open up vistas of all we and
they will do, when this new power we strive
for is attained. If we are tempted down that
vista we find with shame after an hour of
vain musing that we were lured away, had
deserted our task and forgotten that stern
fixity of the will we set out to achieve. Let
us persevere in our daily ritual and the
turmoil increases ; our whole being becomes
vitalised, the bad as well as the good. The
heat of this fervent concentration acts like
fire under a pot, and everything in our being
boils up madly. We learn our own hitherto
unknown character. We did not know we
could feel such fierce desires, never imagined
such passionate enmities as now awaken.
We have created in ourselves a centre of
power and grow real to ourselves. It is
dangerous, too, for we have flung ourselves
into the eternal conflict between spirit and
matter, and find ourselves where the battle is

hottest, where the foemen are locked in a
death struggle. We are in grips with mightier
powers than we had before conceived of.
What man is there who thinks he has self-
control? He stands in the shallow waters,
nor has gone into the great deep, nor been
tossed at the mercy of the waves. Let him
rouse the arcane powers in himself, and he
will feel like one who has let loose the
avalanche. None would live through that
turmoil if the will were the only power in
ourselves we could invoke, for the will is
neither good nor bad but is power only, and
it vitalises good or bad indifferently. If that
were all our labour would bring us, not
closer to divine being, but only to a dilation
of the personality. But the ancients who
taught us to gain this intensity taught it but
as preliminary to a meditation which would
not waver and would be full of power. The
meditation they urged on us has been explained as " the inexpressible yearning of the
inner man to go out into the infinite." But
that Infinite we would enter is living. It is
the ultimate being of us. Meditation is a
fiery brooding on that majestical Self. We
imagine ourselves into Its vastness. We conceive ourselves as mirroring Its infinitudes,

as moving in all things, as living in all beings, in earth, water, air, fire, æther. We try to know as It knows, to live as It lives, to be compassionate as It is compassionate. We equal ourselves to It that we may understand It and become It. We do not kneel to It as slaves, but as Children of the King we lift ourselves up to that Glory, and affirm to ourselves that we are what we imagine. "What a man thinks, that he is : that is the old secret," said the wise. We have imagined ourselves into this pitiful dream of life. By imagination and will we re-enter true being, becoming that we conceive of. On that path of fiery brooding I entered. At first all was stupor. I felt as one who steps out of day into the colourless night of a cavern, and that was because I had suddenly reversed the habitual motions of life. We live normally seeing through the eyes, hearing through the ears, stirred by the senses, moved by bodily powers, and receiving only such spiritual knowledge as may pass through a momentary purity of our being. On the mystic path we create our own light, and at first we struggle blind and baffled, seeing nothing, hearing nothing, unable to think, unable to imagine. We seem deserted by dream, vision or in-

spiration, and our meditation barren altogether. But let us persist through weeks or
months, and sooner or later that stupor disappears. Our faculties readjust themselves,
and do the work we will them to do.
Never did they do their work so well. The
dark caverns of the brain begin to grow
luminous. We are creating our own light.
By heat of will and aspiration we are trans-
muting what is gross in the subtle æthers
through which the mind works. As the
dark bar of metal begins to glow, at
first redly, and then at white heat, or as ice
melts and is alternately fluid, vapour, gas,
and at last a radiant energy, so do these
æthers become purified and alchemically
changed into luminous essences, and they
make a new vesture for the soul, and link us
to mid-world or heavenward where they too
have their true home. How quick the mind
is now! How vivid is the imagination!
We are lifted above the tumult of the body.
The heat of the blood disappears below us.
We draw nigher to ourselves. The heart
longs for the hour of meditation and hurries
to it ; and, when it comes, we rise within ourselves as a diver too long under seas rises
to breathe the air, to see the light. We have

invoked the God and we are answered according to old promise. As our aspiration so is our inspiration. We imagine It as Love and what a love enfolds us. We conceive of It as Might and we take power from that Majesty. We dream of It as Beauty and the Magician of the Beautiful appears everywhere at Its miraculous art, and the multitudinous lovely creatures of Its thought are busy moulding nature and life in their image, and all are hurrying, hurrying to the Golden World. This vision brings its own proof to the spirit, but words cannot declare or explain it. We must go back to lower levels and turn to that which has form from that which is bodiless.

THE MANY-COLOURED LAND

I HAVE always been curious about the psychology of my own vision as desirous of imparting it, and I wish in this book to relate the efforts of an artist and poet to discover what truth lay in his own imaginations. I have brooded longer over the nature of imagination than I have lingered over the canvas where I tried to rebuild my vision. Spiritual moods are difficult to express and cannot be argued over, but the workings of imagination may well be spoken of, and need precise and minute investigation. I surmise from my reading of the psychologists who treat of this that they themselves were without this faculty and spoke of it as blind men who would fain draw although without vision. We are overcome when we read *Prometheus Unbound*, but who, as he reads, flings off the enchantment to ponder in what state was the soul of Shelley in that ecstasy of swift

creation.   Who has questioned the artist to
whom the forms of his thought are vivid as
the forms of nature ?   Artist and poet have
rarely been curious about the processes of their
own minds.   Yet it is reasonable to assume
that the highest ecstasy and vision are
conditioned by law and attainable by all, and
this might be argued as of more importance
even than the message of the seers.   I attribute
to that unwavering meditation and fiery concentration of will a growing luminousness in
my brain as if I had unsealed in the body a
fountain of interior light.   Normally we close
our eyes on a cloudy gloom through which
vague forms struggle sometimes into definite-
ness.   But the luminous quality gradually
became normal in me, and at times in meditation there broke in on me an almost intolerable
lustre of light, pure and shining faces, dazzling
processions of figures, most ancient, ancient
places and peoples, and landscapes lovely as
the lost Eden.   These appeared at first to
have no more relation to myself than images
from a street without one sees reflected in a
glass ; but at times meditation prolonged
itself into spheres which were radiant with
actuality.   Once, drawn by some inner impulse
to meditate at an unusual hour, I found quick

oblivion of the body. The blood and heat of the brain ebbed from me as an island fades in the mists behind a swift vessel fleeting into light. The ways were open within. I rose through myself and suddenly felt as if I had awakened from dream. Where was I? In what city? Here were hills crowned with glittering temples, and the ways, so far as I could see, were thronged with most beautiful people, swaying as if shaken by some ecstasy running through all as if the Dark Hidden Father was breathing rapturous life within His children. Did I wear to them an aspect like their own? Was I visible to them as a new-comer in their land of lovely light? I could not know, but those nigh me flowed towards me with outstretched hands. I saw eyes with a beautiful flame of love in them looking into mine. But I could stay no longer for something below drew me down and I was again an exile from light.

There came through meditation a more powerful orientation of my being as if to a hidden sun, and my thoughts turned more and more to the spiritual life of Earth. All the needles of being pointed to it. I felt instinctively that all I saw in vision was part of the life of Earth which is a court where there

are many starry palaces.   There the Planetary
Spirit was King, and that Spirit manifesting
through the substance of Earth, the Mighty
Mother, was, I felt, the being I groped after
as God.   The love I had for nature as
garment of that deity grew deeper.   That
which was my own came to me as it comes to
all men.   That which claimed me drew me to
itself.   I had my days and nights of freedom.
How often did I start in the sunshine of a
Sabbath morning, setting my face to the hills,
feeling somewhat uncertain as a lover who
draws nigh to a beauty he adores, who sometimes will yield everything to him and
sometimes is silent and will only endure his
presence.   I did not know what would happen
to me, but I was always expectant, and walked
up to the mountains as to the throne of God.
Step by step there fell from me the passions
and fears of the week-day, until, as I reached
the hillside and lay on the grassy slope with
shut eyes, I was bare of all but desire for the
Eternal.   I was once more the child close to
the Mother.   She rewarded me by lifting for
me a little the veil which hides her true face.
To those high souls who know their kinship
the veil is lifted, her face is revealed, and
her face is like a bride's.   Petty as was my

everyday life, with the fears and timidities which abnormal sensitiveness begets, in those moments of vision I understood instinctively the high mood they must keep who would walk with the highest ; and who with that divine face glimmering before him could do aught but adore !

There is an instinct which stills the lips which would speak of mysteries whose day for revelation has not drawn nigh. The little I know of these I shall not speak of. It is always lawful to speak of that higher wisdom which relates our spiritual being to that multitudinous unity which is God and Nature and Man. The only justification for speech from me, rather than from others whose knowledge is more profound, is that the matching of words to thoughts is an art I have practised more. What I say may convey more of truth, as the skilled artist, painting a scene which he views for the first time, may yet suggest more beauty and enchantment than the habitual dweller, unskilled in art, who may yet know the valley he loves so intimately that he could walk blindfold from end to end.

I do not wish to write a book of wonders, but rather to bring thought back to that Being

whom the ancient seers worshipped as Deity.
I believe that most of what was said of God
was in reality said of that Spirit whose body
is Earth.   I must in some fashion indicate
the nature of the visions which led me to
believe with Plato that the earth is not at all
what the geographers suppose it to be, and
that we live like frogs at the bottom of a
marsh knowing nothing of that Many-Coloured
Earth which is superior to this we know, yet
related to it as soul to body.   On that Many-
Coloured Earth, he tells us, live a divine folk,
and there are temples wherein the gods do
truly dwell, and I wish to convey, so far as
words may, how some apparitions of that
ancient beauty came to me in wood or on
hillside or by the shores of the western
sea.

Sometimes lying on the hillside with the
eyes of the body shut as in sleep I could see
valleys and hills, lustrous as a jewel, where
all was self-shining, the colours brighter and
purer, yet making a softer harmony together
than the colours of the world I know.   The
winds sparkled as they blew hither and thither,
yet far distances were clear through that
glowing air.   What was far off was precise
as what was near, and the will to see hurried

me to what I desired. There, too, in that land I saw fountains as of luminous mist jetting from some hidden heart of power, and shining folk who passed into those fountains inhaled them and drew life from the magical air. They were, I believe, those who in the ancient world gave birth to legends of nymph and dryad. Their perfectness was like the perfectness of a flower, a beauty which had never, it seemed, been broken by act of the individualised will which with us makes possible a choice between good and evil, and the marring of the mould of natural beauty. More beautiful than we they yet seemed less than human, and I surmised I had more thoughts in a moment than they through many of their days. Sometimes I wondered had they individualised life at all, for they moved as if in some orchestration of their being. If one looked up, all looked up. If one moved to breathe the magical airs from the fountains, many bent in rhythm. I wondered were their thoughts all another's, one who lived within them, guardian or oversoul to their tribe?

Like these were my first visions of super-nature, not spiritual nor of any high import, not in any way so high as those transcendental moments of awe, when almost without vision the Divine Darkness seemed to breathe within the spirit. But I was curious about these forms, and often lured away by them from the highest meditation ; for I was dazzled like a child who escapes from a dark alley in one of our cities of great sorrow where its life has been spent, and who comes for the first time upon some rich garden beyond the city where the air is weighted with scent of lilac or rose, and the eyes are made gay with colour. Such a beauty begins to glow on us as we journey towards Deity, even as earth grows brighter as we journey from the gloomy pole to lands of the sun ; and I would cry out to our humanity, sinking deeper into the Iron Age, that the Golden World is all about us and that beauty is open to all, and none are shut out from it who will turn to it and seek for it.

As the will grew more intense, the longing for the ancestral self more passionate, there came glimpses of more rapturous life in the being of Earth. Once I lay on the sand dunes by the western sea. The air seemed filled with melody. The motion of the wind made a continuous musical vibration. Now and then the silvery sound of bells broke on my ear. I saw nothing for a time. Then there was an intensity of light before my eyes like the flashing of sunlight through a crystal. It widened like the opening of a gate and I saw the light was streaming from the heart of a glowing figure. Its body was pervaded with light as if sunfire rather than blood ran through its limbs. Light streams flowed from it. It moved over me along the winds, carrying a harp, and there was a circling of golden hair that swept across the strings. Birds flew about it, and over the brows was a fiery plumage as of wings of outspread flame. On the face was an ecstasy of beauty and immortal youth. There were others, a lordly folk, and they passed by on the wind as if they knew me not or the earth I lived on. When I came back to myself my own world seemed grey and devoid of light though the summer sun was hot upon the sands.

One other vision I will tell because it bears on things the ancients taught us, and on what I have to write in later pages. Where I saw this I will not say. There was a hall vaster than any cathedral, with pillars that seemed built out of living and trembling opal, or from some starry substances which shone with every colour, the colours of eve and dawn. A golden air glowed in this place, and high between the pillars were thrones which faded, glow by glow, to the end of the vast hall. On them sat the Divine Kings. They were fire-crested. I saw the crest of the dragon on one, and there was another plumed with brilliant fires that jetted forth like feathers of flame. They sat shining and starlike, mute as statues, more colossal than Egyptian images of their gods, and at the end of the hall was a higher throne on which sat one greater than the rest. A light like the sun glowed behind him. Below on the floor of the hall lay a dark figure as if in trance, and two of the Divine Kings made motions with their hands about it over head and body. I saw where their hands waved how sparkles of fire like the flashing of jewels broke out. There rose out of that dark body a figure as tall, as glorious, as shining as those seated on the thrones. As he woke to the hall he became aware of his divine kin, and he lifted up his hands in greeting. He had returned from his pilgrimage through darkness, but now an initiate, a master in the heavenly guild. While he gazed on

them the tall golden figures from their
thrones leaped up, they too with hands uplifted in greeting, and they passed from me
and faded swiftly in the great glory behind
the throne.

ANALYTIC

BEFORE I may write more of that supernature which rises, a tower of heaven, above the depths where we move, I know I must try to solve some of the doubts and perplexities which come to most who hear of things they have not heard or seen for their own part. They will say, " You are an artist and have painted such things. We know you have imagination which creates images vividly. You are a poet, and it is the art of your tribe to gild for us the thoughts you have, the emotions you feel, so that what moods are common with us you attire richly till they walk like kings. But what certainty have you that it is not all fancy, and the visions you speak of were not born in the cloudy hollows of your brain, and are not glorified memories of things you have first seen with the sensual eye, and which were afterwards refashioned in memory ? What certitude have you that these things you speak of are in any way related to a real world invisible to our eyes ?" To solve these doubts I must not fall back on authority, or appeal for trust. It will avail nothing to say that others have seen such things and have with me looked upon them, we speaking of them together as people who see the same scene, who refer as they speak to rocks, waters and trees, knowing these are a common vision. It would be true if I said this, but it would avail me nothing in my desire that you should go hopefully on the way I would have you journey. On that path, as an ancient scripture says, to whatsoever place one would travel that place one's own self becomes, and I must try first to uproot false ideas about memory, imagination and vision so that by pure reason people may be led out of error and be able to distinguish between that which arises in themselves and that which comes otherwise and which we surmise is a visitor from a far country. I too in boyhood had the idea so commonly held that the pictures of imagination are old memories refashioned. I first doubted this as a child when, lying on my bed, there came a sudden illumination of my brain, and pictures moved before my inner eyes like the coloured

moving pictures we see in the theatre.   I saw,
I remember, a sunlit hillside which seemed
close to me.   There were huge grey boulders
strewn about.   Beyond this hill-slope I could
see far distant mountains, pale blue through
the sparkling air.   While I looked, giants in
brazen armour clambered swiftly up the hillside, swinging clubs which had spiked balls of
brass held by a chain at the end.   They
glittered in the sun as they ran up and past
me.   Motion, light, shadow, colour were
perfect as things seen passing before the
physical eyes.   Then the illumination in my
brain ceased, the picture vanished, and I was
startled, for I had seen no hillside like that,
no distant mountains, no giants in brazen
armour in picture or theatre, and I began a
speculation which soon ended because childhood keeps no prolonged meditation.   I may
take this as a type of vision common to most
people.   Either when they sit in darkness,
or with closed eyes, or as they drift into sleep
or awaken from sleep, they pass through
strange cities, float in the air, roam through
woods, have adventures with people who are
not the people they meet every day.   There
is nothing uncommon about such visions.
It is in the interpretation of them that error

arises.　People pass them by too easily saying,
" It is imagination," as if imagination were
as easily explained as a problem in Euclid,
and was not a mystery, and as if every moving
picture in the brain did not need such minute
investigation as Darwin gave to earthworms.
I was asked to believe that giants, armour,
hillside and sunny distance so appeared in my
brain because I had seen men who might be
enlarged to giants, pictures of armour with
which they could be clothed by fancy, brass
with which the armour could be coloured.
Any rocks might be multiplied and enlarged
from memory by imagination to form a hillside,
and any sky of sunny blue would make my
distance.　How plausible for a second !　How
unthinkable after a momentary consideration !
I know I could hardly, if you gave me a
hundred thousand pictures of heads, by cutting
them up and pasting them together, make a
fresh face which would appear authentic in
its tints and shadows, and it would be a work
of infinite labour.　But these faces of vision
are not still.　They move.　They have life
and expression.　The sunlight casts authentic
moving shadows on the ground.　What is
it combines with such miraculous skill the
things seen, taking a tint here, a fragment of

form there, which uses the colours and forms
of memory as a palette to paint such master-
pieces ?   It has been said, " Every man is a
Shakespeare in his dreams."   The dreamer of
landscape is more than a Turner, because he
makes his trees to bend before the wind and
his clouds to fleet across the sky.   The waking
brain does not do this.   It is unconscious of
creation.   To say we refashion memories is
to surmise in the subconscious nature a
marvellous artist, to whom all that we have
ever seen with the physical eyes is present at
once, and as clay in the hands of a divine
potter, and it is such swift creation too that
it rivals the works of the Lord.   Well, I am
not one of those who deny that the Kingdom
of Heaven is within us or that the King is
also in His Heaven.   We need not deny that
and yet hold that vision comes otherwise.
Nor can be it denied that vision is often so
radiant and precise, for experience affirms that
it is, and hundreds of artists, and indeed
people who are not artists at all, will tell you
how clearly they see in their dreams.   But
for those who hold that visions such as I and
many others have had are only the refashioning
of memory, and there is nothing mysterious
about them, I say try to think out tint by

tint, form by form, how these could be recombined, and, for whatever marvel I would have you believe, you will have substituted something just as marvellous but not so credible. Not that it is incredible to think that the spirit in man is Creator, for all the prophets and seers of the world have told us that, but the common psychological explanation is not acceptable, because we know that forms can appear in the brain which were transferred by will from one person to another. When we know that, when we know this inner eye can see the form in another's mind, we must regard it as indicating an immense possibility of vision on that plane. We then ask ourselves concerning all these strange cities and landscapes of dream, all these impish faces which flout at us when we are drowsy, all these visions living and moving in our minds, whether they too came, not by way of the physical senses transformed in memory, but came like the image thought transferred, or by obscure ways reflected from spheres above us, from the lives of others and the visions of others. If we brood on this we will come to think the old explanation is untenable and will address ourselves with wonder and hope to the exploration of this strange country within ourselves, and will try to find out its limits, and whether from image or vision long pondered over we may not reach to their original being.

I think few of our psychologists have had imagination themselves. They have busy brains, and, as an Eastern proverb says, " The broken water surface reflects only broken images." They see too feebly to make what they see a wonder to themselves. They discuss the mode of imagination as people might discuss art, who had never seen painting or sculpture. One writer talks about light being a vibration, and the vibration affecting the eye and passing along the nerves until it is stored up in the brain cells. The vibration is, it appears, stayed or fixed there. Yet I know that every movement of mine, the words I speak, the circulation of my blood, cause every molecule in my body to vibrate. How is this vibration in the cells unaffected? It must remain unaffected in their hypothesis, for I can recall the original scene, can discuss it, can after years re-summon it again and find the image clear as at first. I refer to it in thought and it remains unchanged. The physical explana-tion of memory itself breaks down even as the material explanation of imagination breaks down. Can an unchanging vibration be retained when the substance which holds the vibration is itself subject to continual movement? The moment we close our eyes and are alone with our thoughts and the pictures of dream, we are alone with mystery and miracle. Or are we alone? Are we secure there from intrusion? Are we not nearer the thronged highways of existence where gods, demons, men and goblins all are psychical visitors. I will not speak here of high things because I am trying to argue with people who see no wonder in anything, and dismiss all high things with a silly phrase as fancy or imagination or hallucination. But I know from questioning many people that it is common with them before they sleep to see faces, while their eyes are closed, and they are, as they think, alone. These faces are sometimes the faces of imps who frown at them, put out their tongues at them, grin or gibber. Sometimes not a face but a figure, or figures, will be seen which, like the faces, seem endowed with life. To call this imagination or fancy is to explain nothing because the explanation is not explained. The more one concentrates on these most trivial mental apparitions, the more certain do we feel they have a life of their own, and that our brain is as full of living creatures as our body is thronged with tiny cells, each a life, or as the blood may swarm with bacteria. I draw attention to the mystery in obvious and common things, and ask that they be explained and not slurred over as if no explanation were necessary. I ask the doubters of my vision to penetrate a little into the mystery of their own thoughts and dreams before they cry out against me, who for many years travelled far and came upon lovely and inhabited regions to which I would also lead them. I know that my brain is a court where many living creatures throng, and I am never alone in it. You, too, can know that if you heighten the imagination and intensify the will. The darkness in you will begin to glow, and you will see clearly, and you will know that what you thought was but a mosaic of memories is rather the froth of a gigantic ocean of life, breaking on the shores of matter, casting up its own flotsam to mingle with the life of the shores it breaks on. If you will light your lamp you can gaze far over that ocean and even embark on it. Sitting in your chair you can travel farther than ever Columbus travelled and to lordlier worlds than his eyes had rested on. Are you not tired of surfaces ? Come with me and we will bathe in the Fountains of Youth. I can point you the way to El Dorado.

THE MINGLING OF NATURES

To move a single step we must have power.
To see we must be exalted. Not to be lost
in vision we must learn the geography of the
spirit and the many mansions in the being of
the Father. If we concentrate we shall have
power. If we meditate we shall lift ourselves
above the dark environment of the brain.
The inner shall become richer and more
magical to us than the outer which has held
us so long. How may I allure to this
meditation those who see only by the light
of day ; who, when their eyes are shut, are
as cave-dwellers living in a blackness beneath
the hills ? The cave of the body can be lit
up. If we explore it we shall there find
lights by which the lights of day are made
dim. I perhaps to build on had some little
gift of imagination I brought with me into
the world, but I know others who had no
natural vision who acquired this, and by

sustained meditation and by focussing the
will to a burning-point, were raised above
the narrow life of the body. Being an
artist and a lover of visible beauty, I was
often tempted from the highest meditation
to contemplate, not divine being, but the
mirage of forms. Yet because I was so
bewitched and was curious about all I saw,
I was made certain that the images which
populate the brain have not always been there,
nor are refashioned from things seen. I
know that with the pictures of memory
mingle pictures which come to us, sometimes
from the minds of others, sometimes are
glimpses of distant countries, sometimes
are reflections of happenings in regions invisible to the outer eyes ; and as meditation
grows more exalted, the forms traceable to
memory tend to disappear and we have access
to a memory greater than our own, the
treasure-house of august memories in the in-
numerable being of Earth. When minute
analysis is made of images in the brain, those
foolish fables about memory and imagination
no longer affect those who begin this quest,
and we see how many streams are tributary
to our life. All I have said may be proved
by any as curious about things of the mind

as I was, if they will but light the candle on
their forehead and examine the denizens in
the brain.   They will find that their sphere
is populous with the innermost thoughts of
others, and will more and more be led by
wonder and awe to believe that we and all
things swim in an æther of deity, and that
the least motion of our minds is incomprehensible except in memory of this : " In
Him we live and move and have our being."
Analysis of the simplest mental apparition
will lead us often to stay ourselves on that
thought.   Once in an idle interval in my
work I sat with my face pressed in my hands,
and in that dimness pictures began flickering
in my brain.   I saw a little dark shop, the
counter before me, and behind it an old man
fumbling with some papers, a man so old
that his motions had lost swiftness and precision.   Deeper in the store was a girl, red-
haired, with grey watchful eyes fixed on the
old man.   I saw that to enter the shop one
must take two steps downwards from a
cobbled pavement without.   I questioned
a young man, my office companion, who
then was writing a letter, and I found that
what I had seen was his father's shop.
All my imaginations—the old man, his

yellow-white beard, his fumbling movements,
the watchful girl, her colour, the steps, the
cobbled pavement—were not imaginations of
mine in any true sense, for while I was in a
vacant mood my companion had been thinking of his home, and his brain was populous
with quickened memories, and they invaded
my own mind, and when I made question I
found their origin.   But how many thousand
times are we invaded by such images and
there is no speculation over them ?   Possibly
I might have made use of such things in my
art.   I might have made a tale about the old
man and girl.   But if I had done so, if other
characters had appeared in my tale who
seemed just as living, where would they have
come from ?   Would I have again been
drawing upon the reservoir of my companion's
memories ?   The vision of the girl and old
man may in reality have been but a little
part of the images with which my brain was
flooded.   Did I then see all, or might not
other images in the same series emerge at
some later time and the connection be lost ?
If I had written a tale and had imagined an
inner room, an old mother, an absent son,
a family trouble, might I not all the while be
still adventuring in another's life ?   While

we think we are imagining a character we may, so marvellous are the hidden ways, be really interpreting a being actually existing, brought into psychic contact with us by some affinity of sentiment or soul.

I brooded once upon a friend not then knowing where he was, and soon I seemed to myself to be walking in the night. Nigh me was the Sphinx, and, more remote, a dim pyramid. Months later my friend came to Ireland. I found he had been in Egypt at the time I had thought of him. He could not recollect the precise day, but had while there spent a night beside the great monuments. I did not see him in vision, but I seemed to be walking there in the night. Why did the angle of vision change as with one moving about? Did I see through his eyes? Or did I see, as in the other incident, images reflected from his sphere to my own? Where does this vision end? What are its limitations? Would we, fully come to ourselves, be like those beings in the Apocalypse full of eyes within and without? Would we, in the fulness of power, act through many men and speak through many voices? Were Shakespeare and the great masters unconscious magi, blind visionaries, feeling and comprehending a life they could not see, or who, if they saw, thought it was their own creation. We must ask ourselves these questions, for, when our lamp is lit, we find the house of our being has many chambers, and creatures live there who come and go, and we must ask whether they have the right to be in our house ; and there are corridors there leading into the hearts of others, and windows which open into eternity, and we hardly can tell where our own being ends and another begins, or if there is any end to our being. If we brood with love upon this myriad unity, following the meditation ordained by Buddha for the brothers of his order, to let our minds pervade the whole wide world with heart of love, we come more and more to permeate, or to be pervaded by the lives of others. We are haunted by unknown comrades in many moods, whose naked souls pass through ours, and reveal themselves to us in an un-forgettable instant, and we know them as we hardly know those who are the daily comrades of our heart, who, however intimate, are hidden from us by the husk of the body. As the inner life grows richer we beget more of these affinities. We wonder what relation with them is rightly ours. Do we affect them by a sympathy unknown to them as they move us by a revelation more intimate than could be uttered by words? We discover in ourselves a new sense. By touch with the soul we understand. We realise how profound was that ancient wisdom which told us when we were perfected in concentration we could gain full comprehension of anything we wished by intent brooding. I never attained that perfectness of concentration, but I saw the possibilities in moments of electric intensity of will when I summoned out of the past a knowledge I desired. How is this knowledge possible? Is there a centre within us through which all the threads of the universe are drawn, a spiritual atom which mirrors the spiritual infinitudes even as the eye is a mirror of the external heavens? There is not a pin point in visible space which does not contain a microcosm of heaven and earth. We know that, for nowhere do we move where the eye does not receive its vision of infinity. Is it only in the visible world, this condensation of the infinite in the atomic, and not also in the soul and again in the spirit? What would the soul in its perfection mirror?

Would it reflect within itself the myriad life of humanity ? Would the spirit mirror the heavens, and the imaginations of the Divine Mind well up within it in mystic and transcendental ideations ? Or do they already mirror each their own world, and is all knowledge already within us, and is our need but for wisdom to create the links between portions of a single being, dramatically sundered by illusion as the soul is in dream ? Is not the gathering of the will and the fiery brooding to this end, and are the glimpses we get of supernature caused but by the momentary uplifting of an eye, by which, when it is fully awakened, we dead shall be raised ?

THE MEMORY OF EARTH

WE experience the romance and delight of
voyaging upon uncharted seas when the
imagination is released from the foolish notion
that the images seen in reverie and dream are
merely the images of memory refashioned ;
and in tracking to their originals the forms
seen in vision we discover for them a varied
ancestry, as that some come from the minds
of others, and of some we cannot surmise
another origin than that they are portions of
the memory of Earth which is accessible to
us. We soon grow to think our memory
but a portion of that eternal memory and
that we in our lives are gathering an innumer-
able experience for a mightier being than our
own. The more vividly we see with the
inner eye the more swiftly do we come to
this conviction. Those who see vaguely are
satisfied with vague explanations which those
who see vividly at once reject as inadequate.

How are we to explain what has happened to many, and oftentimes to myself, that when we sit amid ancient ruins or in old houses they renew their life for us ? I waited for a friend inside a ruined chapel and while there a phantasm of its ancient uses came vividly before me. In front of the altar I saw a little crowd kneeling, most prominent a woman in a red robe, all pious and emotionally intent. A man stood behind these leaning by the wall as if too proud to kneel. An old man in ecclesiastical robes, abbot or bishop, stood, a crozier in one hand, while the other was uplifted in blessing or in emphasis of his words. Behind the cleric a boy carried a vessel, and the lad's face was vain with self-importance. I saw all this suddenly as if I was contemporary and was elder in the world by many centuries. I could surmise the emotional abandon of the red-robed lady, the proud indifference of the man who stood with his head but slightly bent, the vanity of the young boy as servitor in the ceremony, just as in a church to-day we feel the varied mood of those present. Anything may cause such pictures to rise in vivid illumination before us, a sentence in a book, a word, or contact with some object. I have brooded

over the grassy mounds which are all that
remain of the duns in which our Gaelic
ancestors lived, and they builded themselves
up again for me so that I looked on what
seemed an earlier civilisation, saw the people,
noted their dresses, the colours of natural
wool, saffron or blue, how rough like our
own homespuns they were ; even such
details were visible as that the men cut meat
at table with knives and passed it to the lips
with their fingers.   This is not, I am convinced, what people call imagination, an
interior creation in response to a natural
curiosity about past ages.   It is an act of
vision, a perception of images already existing
breathed on some ethereal medium which in
no way differs from the medium which holds
for us our memories ; and the reperception
of an image in memory which is personal to
us in no way differs as a psychical act from
the perception of images in the memory of
Earth.   The same power of seeing is turned
upon things of the same character and substance.   It is not only rocks and ruins which
infect us with such visions.   A word in a
book when one is sensitive may do this also.
I sought in a classical dictionary for informa-
tion about some myth.   What else on the

page my eye caught I could not say, but something there made two thousand years to vanish. I was looking at the garden of a house in some ancient city. From the house into the garden fluttered two girls, one in purple and the other in a green robe, and they, in a dance of excitement, ran to the garden wall and looked beyond it to the right. There a street rose high to a hill where there was a pillared building. I could see through blinding sunlight a crowd swaying down the street drawing nigh the house, and the two girls were as excited as girls might be to-day if king or queen were entering their city. This instant uprising of images following a glance at a page cannot be explained as the refashioning of the pictures of memory. The time which elapsed after the page was closed and the apparition in the brain was a quarter of a minute or less. One can only surmise that pictures so vividly coloured, so full of motion and sparkle as are moving pictures in the theatres were not an instantaneous creation by some magical artist within us, but were evoked out of a vaster memory than the personal, that the Grecian names my eye had caught had the power of symbols which evoke their affinities, and the picture

of the excited girls and the shining procession
was in some fashion, I know not how, connected with what I had read. We cannot
pass by the uprising of these images with
some vague phrase about suggestion or
imagination and shirk further inquiry. If
with the physical eye twenty-five years ago a
man had seen a winged aeroplane amid the
clouds it had roused him to a tumult of
speculation and inquiry. But if the same
picture had been seen in the mind it would
speedily have been buried as mere fancy.
There would have been no speculation, though
what appears within us might well be deemed
more important than what appears without
us. Every tint, tone, shape, light or shade
in an interior image must have intelligible
cause as the wires, planes, engines and pro-
pellers of the aeroplane have. We must
infer, when the image is clear and precise,
an original of which this is the reflection.
Whence or when were the originals of the
pictures we see in dream or reverie ? There
must be originals ; and, if we are forced to
dismiss as unthinkable any process by which
the pictures of our personal memory could
unconsciously be reshaped into new pictures
which appear in themselves authentic copies

of originals, which move, have light, colour, form, shade such as nature would bestow, then we are led to believe that memory is an attribute of all living creatures and of Earth also, the greatest living creature we know, and that she carries with her, and it is accessible to us, all her long history, cities far gone behind time, empires which are dust, or are buried with sunken continents beneath the waters. The beauty for which men perished is still shining; Helen is there in her Troy, and Deirdre wears the beauty which blasted the Red Branch. No ancient lore has perished. Earth retains for herself and her children what her children might in passion have destroyed, and it is still in the realm of the Ever Living to be seen by the mystic adventurer. We argue that this memory must be universal, for there is nowhere we go where Earth does not breathe fragments from her ancient story to the meditative spirit. These memories gild the desert air where once the proud and golden races had been and had passed away, and they haunt the rocks and mountains where the Druids evoked their skiey and subterrene deities. The laws by which this history is made accessible to us seem to be the same as

those which make our own learning swift to
our service.   When we begin thought or
discussion on some subject we soon find ourselves thronged with memories ready for use.
Everything in us related by affinity to the
central thought seems to be mobilised ; and
in meditation those alien pictures we see, not
the pictures of memory, but strange scenes,
cities, beings and happenings, are, if we study
them, all found to be in some relation to our
mood.   If our will is powerful enough and if
by concentration and aspiration we have made
the gloom in the brain to glow, we can evoke
out of the memory of earth images of whatsoever we desire.   These earth memories
come to us in various ways.   When we are
passive, and the ethereal medium which is
the keeper of such images, not broken up by
thought, is like clear glass or calm water,
then there is often a glowing of colour and
form upon it, and there is what may be a
reflection from some earth memory connected
with the place we move in or it may be we
have direct vision of that memory.   Meditation again evokes images and pictures which
are akin to its subject and our mood and
serve in illustration of it.   Once, when I was
considering the play of arcane forces in the

body, a book appeared before me, a coloured symbol on each page. I saw the book was magical, for while I looked on one of these the symbol vanished from the page, and the outline of a human body appeared, and then there came an interior revelation of that, and there was a shining of forces and a flashing of fires, rose, gold, azure and silver along the spinal column, and these flowed up into the brain where they struck upon a little ball that was like white sunfire for brilliancy, and they flashed out of that again in a pulsation as of wings on each side of the head ; and then the page darkened, and the changing series closed with the Caduceus of Mercury and contained only a symbol once more.

Such pictures come without conscious effort of will, but are clearly evoked by it. Lastly, but more rarely with me, because the electric intensity of will required was hard to attain, I was able at times to evoke deliberately out of the memory of nature pictures of persons or things long past in time, but of which I desired knowledge. I regret now, while I was young and my energies yet uncoiled, that I did not practise this art of evocation more in regard to matters where knowledge might be regarded as of spiritual value ; but I was like a child who discovers a whole set of fresh toys, and plays with one after the other, and I was interested in all that came to me, and was too often content to be the servant of my vision and not its master. It was an excitement of spirit for one born in a little country town in Ireland to find the circle of being widened so that life seemed to dilate into a paradise of beautiful memories, and to reach to past ages and to mix with the eternal consciousness of Earth, and when we come on what is new we pause to contemplate it, and do not hurry to the end of our journey. The instances of earth memories given here are trivial in themselves, and they are chosen, not because they are in any way wonderful, but rather because they are like things many people see, and so they may more readily follow my argument. The fact that Earth holds such memories is itself important, for once we discover this imperishable tablet, we are led to speculate whether in the future a training in seership might not lead to a revolution in human knowledge. It is a world where we may easily get lost, and spend hours in futile vision with no more gain than if one looked for long hours at the dust.   For those to whom in their spiritual evolution these apparitions arise I would say : try to become the master of your vision, and seek for and evoke the greatest of earth memories, not those things which only satisfy curiosity, but those which uplift and inspire, and give us a vision of our own greatness ; and the noblest of all Earth's memories is the august ritual of the ancient mysteries, where the mortal, amid scenes of unimaginable grandeur, was disrobed of his mortality and made of the company of the gods.

IMAGINATION

In all I have related hitherto imagination was not present but only vision. These are too often referred to as identical, and in what I have written I have tried to make clear the distinction. If beyond my window I see amid the manifolded hills a river winding ablaze with light, nobody speaks of what is seen as a thing imagined, and if I look out of a window of the soul and see more marvels of shining and shadow, neither is this an act of imagination, which is indeed a higher thing than vision, and a much rarer thing, for in the act of imagination that which is hidden in being, as the Son in the bosom of the Father, is made manifest and a transfiguration takes place like that we imagine in the Spirit when it willed, "Let there be light." Imagination is not a vision of something which already exists, and which in itself must be unchanged by the act of seeing, but by imagination what exists in latency or essence is out-realised and is given a form in thought, and we can contemplate with full consciousness that which hitherto had been unrevealed, or only intuitionally surmised. In imagination there is a revelation of the self to the self, and a definite change in being, as there is in a vapour when a spark ignites it and it becomes an inflammation in the air. Here images appear in consciousness which we may refer definitely to an internal creator, with power to use or remould pre-existing forms, and endow them with life, motion and voice. We infer this because dream and vision sometimes assume a symbolic character and a significance which is personal to us. They tell us plainly, "For you only we exist," and we cannot conceive of what is seen as being a reflection of life in any sphere. In exploring the ancestry of the symbolic vision we draw nigh to that clouded majesty we divine in the depths of our being, and which is heard normally in intuition and conscience, but which now reveals character in its manifestation as the artist in his work. I had a gay adventure when I was a boy at the beginning of my mental travelling, when I met, not a lion, but a symbolic vision in the path. I had read somewhere of one whose dreams made a continuous story from night to night, and I was excited at this and wondered whether I too could not build up life for myself in a fairyland of my own creation, and be the lord of this in dream, and offset the petty circumstance of daily life with the beauty of a realm in which I would be king. I bent myself to this, walking about the country roads at night in the darkness, building up in fantasy the country of sleep. I remember some of my gorgeous fancies. My dream-world was self-shining. Light was born in everything there at dawn, and faded into a coloured gloom at eve, and if I walked across my lawns in darkness the grasses stirred by my feet would waken to vivid colour and glimmer behind me in a trail of green fire ; or if a bird was disturbed at night in my shadowy woods it became a winged jewel of blue, rose, gold and white, and the leaves tipped by its wings would blaze in flakes of emerald flame, and there were flocks of wild birds that my shouts would call forth to light with glittering plumage the monstrous dusk of the heavens. Many other fancies I had which I now forget, and some of them were intuitions about the

Many-Coloured Land. After I had conceived this world, one night in a fury of
effort I willed that it should be my habita-
tion in dream. But of all my dreams I
remember only two. In the first I saw a
mass of pale clouds, and on them was
perched a little ape clutching at the misty
substance with its fingers and trying to
fashion it to some form. It looked from
its work every now and then at something beyond and below the clouds, and I
came closer in my dream and saw that
what the ape was watching was our earth
which spun below in space, and it was trying
to model a sphere of mist in mimicry of that
which spun past it. While I was intent, this
grotesque sculptor turned suddenly, looking
at me with an extraordinary grimace which
said clearly as words could say, "That is
what you are trying to do," and then I was
whirled away again and I was the tiniest
figure in vast mid-air, and before me was a
gigantic gate which seemed lofty as the skies,
and a shadowy figure filled the doorway and
barred my passage. That is all I can remember, and I am forced by dreams like this
to conclude there is a creator of such dreams
within us, for I cannot suppose that anywhere

in space or time a little ape sat on a cloud
and tried to fashion it into planetary form.
The creator of that vision was transcendent
to the waking self and to the self which
experienced the dream, for neither self took
conscious part in the creation.   The creator
of that vision was seer into my consciousness
in waking and in sleep, for what of the vision
I remember was half a scorn of my effort and
half a warning that my ambition was against
natural law.   The creator of that vision could
combine forms and endow them with motion
and life for the vision was intellectual and
penetrated me with its meaning.   Is it ir-
rational to assume so much, or that the
vision indicated a peculiar character in its
creator, and that the ironic mood was not
alien to it nor even humour ?   I am rather
thankful to surmise this of a self which waves
away so many of our dreams and joys, and
which seems in some moods to be remote
from the normal and terrible as the angel
with the flaming sword pointing every way
to guard the Tree of Life.   In this dream
some self of me, higher in the tower of our
being which reaches up to the heavens, made
objective manifestations of its thought ; but
there were moments when it seemed itself to

descend, wrapping its memories of heaven
about it like a cloth, and to enter the body,
and I knew it as more truly myself than that
which began in my mother's womb, and that
it was antecedent to anything which had body
in the world. Here I must return to those
imaginations I had walking about the country
roads as a boy, and select from these, as I
have done from vision, things upon which
the reason may be brought to bear. It is
more difficult, for when there is divine
visitation the mortal is made dark and blind
with glory and, in its fiery fusion with the
spirit, reason is abased or bewildered or
spreads too feeble a net to capture Leviathan,
for often we cannot after translate to ourselves
in memory what the spirit said, though every
faculty is eager to gather what is left after
the visitation even as the rabble in eastern
legend scramble to pick up the gold showered
in the passing of the king. By the time I
was seventeen or eighteen my brain began to
flicker with vivid images. I tried to paint
these, and began with much enthusiasm a
series of pictures which were to illustrate the
history of man from his birth in the Divine
Mind where he glimmered first in the darkness of chaos in vague and monstrous forms

growing ever nigher to the human, to men beasts and men birds, until at last the most perfect form, the divine idea of man, was born in space.   I traced its descent into matter, its conflict with the elements, and finally the series ended in a pessimistic fancy where one of our descendants millions of years hence, a minute philosopher, a creature less than three inches in height, sat on one of our gigantic skulls and watched the skies ruining back into their original chaos and the stars falling from their thrones on the height.   Most of these pictures were only the fancies of a boy, but in considering one of the series I began to feel myself in alliance with a deeper consciousness, and that was when I was trying to imagine the apparition in the Divine Mind of the idea of the Heavenly Man.   Something ancient and eternal seemed to breathe through my fancies. I was blinded then by intensity of feeling to the demerits of the picture, but I was excited in an extraordinary way over what I had done, and I lay awake long into the night brooding over it.   I asked myself what legend I would write under the picture. Something beyond reason held me, and I felt like one who is in a dark room and hears the breathing of another creature, and himself waits breathless for its utterance, and I struggled to understand what wished to be said, and at last, while I was preternaturally dilated and intent, something whispered to me, " Call it the Birth of Aeon." The word " Aeon " thrilled me, for it seemed to evoke by association of ideas, moods and memories most ancient, out of some ancestral life where they lay hidden ; and I think it was the following day that, still meditative and clinging to the word as a lover clings to the name of the beloved, a myth incarnated in me, the story of an Aeon, one of the first starry emanations of Deity, one pre-eminent in the highest heavens, so nigh to Deity and so high in pride that he would be not less than a god himself and would endure no dominion over him save the law of his own will. This Aeon of my imagination revolted against heaven and left its courts, descending into the depths where it mirrored itself in chaos, weaving out of the wild elements a mansion for its spirit. That mansion was our earth and that Aeon was the God of our world. This myth incarnated in me as a boy walking along the country roads in Armagh. I returned to Dublin after a fortnight and it was

a day or two after that I went into the Library
at Leinster House and asked for an art
journal.   I stood by a table while the attend-
ant searched for the volume.   There was a
book lying open there.   My eye rested on it.
It was a dictionary of religions, I think, for
the first word my eye caught was " Aeon "
and it was explained as a word used by the
Gnostics to designate the first created beings.
I trembled through my body.   At that time
I knew nothing of mystical literature and
indeed little of any literature except such tales
as a boy reads, and the imaginations which
had begun to overwhelm me were to me
then nothing but mere imaginations, and were
personal and unrelated in my mind with any
conception of truth, or idea that the imagination could lay hold of truth.   I trembled
because I was certain I had never heard the
word before, and there rushed into my mind
the thought of pre-existence and that this
was memory of the past.   I went away
hurriedly that I might think by myself, but
my thoughts drove me back again soon, and
I asked the librarian who were the Gnostics
and if there was a book which gave an account
of their ideas.   He referred me to a volume of
Neander's *Church History*, and there, in the

section dealing with the Sabaeans, I found the myth of the proud Aeon who mirrored himself in chaos and became the lord of our world. I believed then, and still believe, that the immortal in us has memory of all its wisdom, or, as Keats puts it in one of his letters, there is an ancestral wisdom in man and we can if we wish drink that old wine of heaven. This memory of the spirit is the real basis of imagination, and when it speaks to us we feel truly inspired and a mightier creature than ourselves speaks through us. I remember how pure, holy and beautiful these imaginations seemed, how they came like crystal water sweeping aside the muddy current of my life, and the astonishment I felt, I who was almost inarticulate, to find sentences which seemed noble and full of melody sounding in my brain as if another and greater than I had spoken them ; and how strange it was also a little later to write without effort verse, which some people still think has beauty, while I could hardly, because my reason had then no mastery over the materials of thought, pen a prose sentence intelligently. I am convinced that all poetry is, as Emerson said, first written in the heavens, that is, it is conceived by a self deeper than appears in normal life, and when it speaks to us or tells us its ancient story we taste of eternity and drink the Soma juice, the elixir of immortality.

DREAMS

I HAD discovered through such dreams as that of the satirical ape that there is One who is vigilant through the sleep of the body, and I was led by other dreams to assume that in the heart of sleep there is an intellectual being moving in a world of its own and using transcendental energies. Most of the dreams we remember are chaotic, and these seem often to be determined in character by the accident which brings about our waking. Chaotic as these are, they are full of wonder and miracle, for in the space of a second, almost before a voice has reached the ear of the sleeper or a hand has touched him, some magical engineer has flung a bridge of wild incident over which the spirit races from deep own-being unto outward being. Never when awake could we pack into a second of vivid imagination the myriad incidents that the artificer of dream can create to bring us from the being we remember not back to the dream of life.   This magical swiftness of creation in dream has been noted by many, and those who have had experience of even the most nightmare happenings before waking must be led to surmise that within that blankness we call sleep there is a consciousness in unsleeping vigilance, and this being, which is unsleeping while the body sleeps, excites us to a curiosity as wild as ever led adventurer across uncharted seas.   The ancient seers made earth world, mid-world and heaven world synonyms for three states of consciousness, waking, dreaming and deep sleep.   But the dream state of the soul moving in the mid-world of which they spoke is an intellectual state, and its character is not easily to be guessed from that chaos of fancies we ordinarily remember and call our dreams ; and which I think are not true dreams at all but rather a transitional state on the borderland, like to the froth on the ocean fringes, where there are buffetings of air, churnings of sand, water and weed, while beyond is the pure deep.   I had but slight experience of that loftier life in dream which to others I know was truer life than waking. But none can speak truly of the dreams or imaginations of others, but only of what themselves have known. In intensest meditation I think we encroach on that state which to the waking brain is veiled by sleep and is normally a blank, for in the highest dreams of which I retained memory I was on a plane of being identical with that reached in the apex of meditation and had perceptions of a similar order of things. The black curtain of unconsciousness which drapes the chambers of the brain in sleep, once, for an instant, was magically lifted for me, and I had a glimpse of the high adventures of the unsleeping soul. I found myself floating on the luminous night in a body lighter than air and charged with power, buoyed up above a mountainous region. Beneath me was a wrinkled dusk like the crater of some huge volcano. There were others with me, people with airy glittering bodies, all, like myself, intent on a being mightier than our own. A breath of power poured upward from below as from a fountain, or as if from here some sidereal river flowed out to the country of the stars. We hovered over the fountain from which came that invisible breath filling us with delight and power.   While we hung intent there came the apparition of a vast and glowing orb of light like the radiance about a god, and of those glittering ones some flung themselves into that sphere of light, and were absorbed in it : and it faded away, ebbing from us as if it had been a living galleon come to the hither side of being but for a moment, to carry with it those who might go to the heaven world to be partakers of the divine nature and live in their parent Flame.   I could not cross with that Charon, and I remembered no more, for the curtain of darkness which was magically lifted was again dropped over the chambers of the brain.   But when I woke I was murmuring to myself, as if in interpretation, the words of the Apostle, " We all with open face beholding as in a glass the glory of the Lord are changed unto the same image from glory to glory," and I knew there were many at that mystery who would wake up again outcasts of Heaven, and the God of this world would obliterate memory so that they would never know they had kept tryst with the Kabiri.

Once before, not in dream but in meditation, there had broken in upon me such a

light from the secret places ; and I saw
through earth as through a transparency to
one of those centres of power, "fountains
out of Hecate" as they are called in the
Chaldaic oracles, and which are in the being
of earth, even as in ourselves there are fiery
centres undiscovered by the anatomist where
thought is born or the will leaps up in flame.
And then, and in the dream I have just told,
and in that other vision of the heavenly city
where I found myself among the shining
ones, there seemed to be little of personal
fantasy as there was in the dream of the
ape, but I seemed to myself to be moving
in a real nature which others also have
moved in, and which was perhaps the sphere
known also to that spiritual geographer who
assured Socrates of a many-coloured earth
above this with temples wherein the gods
do truly dwell. I do not wish now to urge
this but only to draw the deductions any
psychologist analysing dream might draw
from dreams not mystical in character. I
may liken myself in my perception of that
dream to a man in a dark hall so utterly
lightless, so soundless, that nothing reaches
him ; and then the door is suddenly flung
open, and he sees a crowd hurrying by, and

then the door is closed and he is again in darkness. Such a man seeing through the door a procession of people in the streets knows they had a life before they came nigh the door and after they passed the door ; and he is not foolish if he speculates on this and how they gathered and for what purpose. So I am justified, I think, in assuming that there was some psychic action in priority to my moment of consciousness. I must seek intellectual causes for events which have logical structure and coherency : I cannot assume that that sudden consciousness of being in the air was absolutely the beginning of that episode any more than I can imagine a flower suddenly appearing without plant or root or prior growth ; nor can I think that blind motions of the brain, in blank unconsciousness of what they tend to, suddenly flame into a consciousness instinct with wild beauty. To assume that would be a freak in reasoning. I might with as much wisdom assume that if in the darkness I took my little son's box of alphabetical bricks, and scattered them about blindly, when the light was turned on I might find that the letters composed a noble sentence. I can reasonably take either of two possibilities, one

being that the dream was self-created fantasy
only, and the other that it was the mirroring
in the brain of an experience of soul in a
real sphere of being. But whether we
assume one or other we postulate an unsleeping consciousness within ourselves while
the brain is asleep : and that unsleeping
creature was either the creator of the dream
or the actor in a real event. Who is that
unsleeping creature ? Is it the same being
who daily inhabits the brain ? Does it rise
up when the body sinks on the couch ? Has
it a dual life as we have when waking, when
half our consciousness is of an external
nature and half of subjective emotions and
thoughts ? Are part of our dreams internal
fantasy and part perceptions of an external
sphere of being ? If I assume that the soul
was an actor in a real event which was
mirrored in the brain, why did I remember
only one moment of the adventure ? To
see any being means that we are on the
same plane. I see you who are physical
because I also have bodily life. If I see an
elemental being or a heavenly being it means
that some part of me is on the same plane
of being or substance. Had I by meditation and concentration evolved in myself

some element akin to that breathed upward
from the mystic fountain, and when the soul
inhaled this fiery essence a rapport began
between free soul and slumbering body, the
circuit was complete, and sleeping and unsleeping being became one ? On that hypothesis there were journeyings of the soul
before and after the moment remembered,
but the action in priority and in succession I
could not remember because there was as
yet no kinship in the brain to the mood of
the unsleeping soul or to the deed it did.
If the soul is an actor in deep sleep, seeing,
hearing and moving in a world of real
energies, then we are justified in assuming a
psychic body within the physical, for to see,
to hear, to move are functions of an organism
however ethereal. Is it the shining of the
Psyche we perceive within ourselves when
through aspiration the body becomes filled
with interior light and consciousness is
steeped in a brilliancy of many colours while
the eyes are closed ? Are we then like the
half-evolved dragon-fly who catches with the
first cracking of its sheath a glimpse of its
own gorgeous plumage ? Was it this body
the prophet spoke of when he said, " Thou
hast been in Eden the Garden of God :

every precious stone was thy covering . . .
thou wast upon the holy mountain of God :
thou hast walked up and down amid the
stones of fire?" And was this spiritual life
lost to man because his heart was lifted up
because of his beauty, and wisdom was cor-
rupted by reason of its own brightness?

If we brood over the alternative that the
dream was self-begotten fantasy, no less
must we make obeisance to the dreamer of
dreams. Who is this who flashes on the
inner eye landscapes as living as those we
see in nature? The winds blow cool upon
the body in dream : the dew is on the
grass : the clouds fleet over the sky : we
float in air and see all things from an angle
of vision of which on waking we have no
experience : we move in unknown cities and
hurry on secret missions. It matters not
whether our dream is a grotesque, the same
marvellous faculty of swift creation is in it.
We are astonished at nightmare happenings
no less than at the lordliest vision, for we
divine in the creation of both the same
magical power. I cannot but think the gnat
to be as marvellous as the Bird of Paradise,
and these twain no less marvellous than
the seraphim. The Master of Life is in all,

and I am as excited with wonder at the creative genius shown in the wildest dream as in the most exalted vision. Not by any power I understand are these images created : but the power which creates them is, I surmise, a mightier self of ours, and yet our slave for purposes of its own. I feel its presence in all I do, think or imagine. It waits on my will. It is in the instant and marvellous marshalling of memories when I speak or write. Out of the myriad chambers of the soul where they lie in latency, an hundred or a thousand memories rise up, words, deeds, happenings, trivial or mighty, the material for thought or speech waiting in due order for use. They sink back silently and are again ready : at the least desire of the will they fly up to consciousness more swiftly than iron filings to the magnet. If I am wakened suddenly I surmise again that it is that enchanter who builds miraculously a bridge of incident to carry me from deep being to outward being. When thought or imagination is present in me, ideas or images appear on the surface of consciousness, and though I call them my thoughts, my imaginations, they are already formed when I become aware of them. The Indian sage Sankara says by

reason of the presence of the highest Self in
us, the mind in us is moved as if moved by
another than ourselves. Upon its presence
depend all motions of body and soul. Could
I embrace even the outer infinitude with the
eye of the body, if it did not preside over
the sense of sight, infinitude interpreting infinitude ? It seems to wait on us as indifferently
and as swiftly when the will in us is evil as
when it is good. It will conjure up for us
images of animalism and lust at the call of
desire. It might speak of itself as the Lord
spoke of Himself to the prophet : " From
me spring forth good and evil." But if we
evoke it for evil it answers with fading
power, and we soon are unable to evoke it
for good, for the evil we have called forth
works for our feebleness and extinction. Or
is there another and evil genie, a dark effigy
of the higher also waiting on us as slave of
our desires ? I do not know. Was it of
the higher it was said, " Ask, and ye shall
receive. Seek, and ye shall find. Knock,
and it shall be opened to you " ? Can
we by searching find out its ways ? Can
we come to an identity of ourselves with
it ? Again I do not know, but the more I
ponder over this unsleeping being, the more

do I feel astonished as Aladdin with lamp or ring, who had but to touch the talisman and a legion of genii were ready to work his will, to build up for him marvellous palaces in the twinkling of an eye, and to ransack for him the treasure-houses of eternity.

THE ARCHITECTURE OF DREAM

I HAVE failed in my purpose if I have not made it clear that in the actual architecture of dream and vision there is a mystery which is not explained by speaking of suppressed desire or sex or any of those springs which modern psychologists surmise are released in dream. A mood may attract its affinities but it does not create what it attracts, and between anger and a definite vision of conflict there is a gulf as mysterious as there was between Aladdin's desire and the building of his marvellous palace. I desire a house, but desire does not build it. I design a house, but every line is drawn with full consciousness, and when I give the plan to the builder every brick is placed with full consciousness by the masons. No coherent architecture in city or dream arises magically by some unreason which translates bodiless desire into organic form. However swift the succession may be, in that second of time between desire and its visionary embodiment or fulfilment there must be space for intellectual labour, the construction of forms or the choice of forms, and the endowing of them with motion.   A second to my brain is too brief a fragment of time for more than sight, but I must believe that to a more intense consciousness, which is co-worker with mine, that second may suffice for a glimpse into some pleroma of form for the selection of these and the unrolling of a vast pageantry.   Something there is, a creature within me, behind whose swiftness I falter a hopeless laggard, for it may be a traveller through the Archaeus and back again with the merchandise of its travel before my pulse has beaten twice.   As an artist who has laboured slowly at the creation of pictures I assert that the forms of dream or vision if self-created require a conscious artist to arrange them, a magician to endow them with life, and that the process is intellectual, that is, it is conscious on some plane of being, though that self which sits in the gate of the body does not know what powers or dignitaries meet in the inner palace chambers of the soul.   When we have

dreams of flying and see all things from an
angle of vision of which we never could
have experience in waking, we know that
to speak of the moving pictures of dream
as memories or unconscious recombinations
of things seen when waking, is to speak
without subtlety or intellectual comprehension. I criticise the figures I see in dream
or vision exactly as I would the figures in
a painting. Even if I see a figure in dream
I have seen when waking, if the figure acts
in a manner differing from its action when
seen with the physical eye, if it now walks
when it then sat, or looks down where before
it looked up, and if these motions in dream
appear authentic so that face and form have
the proper light and shade and the anatomies
are undistorted, that dream change in the
figure of memory is itself a most perplexing
thing. We must suppose that memory
as memory is as fixed in its way as a
sun-picture is fixed or as the attitude
of a statue is fixed. If it fades it should
be by loss of precision and not into other
equally precise but different forms and
gestures. Now we could not without cracks
or distorting of anatomies or complete re-
modelling change the pose of a statue even

if it was modelled in some easily malleable substance ; and the plastic change from stillness to motion in a figure, which we presume to be a memory, is wonderful when we think of it, as wonderful as if the little Tanagra in clay upon my shelf should change from its cast solidity and walk up and down before me. For myself I think man is a protean being, within whose unity there is diversity, and there are creatures in the soul which can inform the images of our memory, or the eternal memory, aye, and speak through them to us in dream, so that we hear their voices, and it is with us in our minute microcosmic fashion even as it was said of the universe that it is a soliloquy of Deity wherein Ain-Soph talks to Ain-Soph.

We can make such general speculations about all pictures moving before the inner eye, and it is always worth while investigating the anatomy of vision and to be intent on what appears to us, for if we have intentness we have memory. A mental picture which at first had yielded nothing to us may be followed by others which indicate a relation to the earliest in the series so that they seem like pages read at different times from the

same book.   When I was young I haunted
the mountains much, finding in the high air
vision became richer and more luminous.   I
have there watched for hours shining landscape and figures in endless procession, trying
to discover in these some significance other
than mere beauty.   Once on the hillside I
seemed to slip from to-day into some remote
yesterday of earth.   There was the same
valley below me, but now it was deepening
into evening and the skies were towering up
through one blue heaven to another.   There
was a battle in the valley and men reeled
darkly hither and thither.   I remember one
warrior about whom the battle was thickest,
for a silver star flickered above his helmet
through the dusk.   But this I soon forgot
for I was impelled to look upwards, and there
above me was an airship glittering with light.
It halted above the valley while a man, grey-
bearded, very majestic, his robes all starred
and jewelled, bent over and looked down
upon the battle.   The pause was but for an
instant, and then the lights flashed more
brilliantly, some luminous mist was jetted
upon the air from many tubes below the boat,
and it soared and passed beyond the mountain,
and it was followed by another and yet others,

all glittering with lights, and they climbed
the air over the hill and were soon lost amid
the other lights of heaven. It must be a
quarter of a century ago since I saw this vision
which I remember clearly because I painted
the ship, and it must, I think, be about five
or six years after that a second vision in the
same series startled me. I was again on the
high places, and this time the apparition in
the mystical air was so close that if I could
have stretched out a hand from this world to
that I could have clutched the aerial voyager
as it swept by me. A young man was steer-
ing the boat, his black hair blown back from
his brows, his face pale and resolute, his head
bent, his eyes intent on his wheel : and beside
him sat a woman, a rose-coloured shawl
speckled with golden threads drawn over her
head, around her shoulders, across her bosom
and folded arms. Her face was proud as a
queen's, and I long remembered that face for
its pride, stillness and beauty. I thought at
the moment it was some image in the eternal
memory of a civilisation more remote than
Atlantis and I cried out in my heart in a
passion of regret for romance passed away
from the world, not knowing that the world's
great age was again returning and that soon

we were to swim once more beneath the epic skies. After that at different times and places I saw other such aerial wanderers, and this I noted, that all such visions had a character in keeping with each other, that they were never mixed up with modernity, that they had the peculiarities by which we recognise civilisations as distinct from each other, Chinese from Greek or Egyptian from Hindu. They were the stuff out of which romance is made, and if I had been a story-teller like our great Standish O'Grady I might have made without questioning a wonder tale of the air, legendary or futurist, but I have always had as much of the philosophic as the artistic interest in what people call imagination, and I have thought that many artists and poets gave to art or romance what would have had an equal if not a greater interest as psychology. I began to ask myself where in the three times or in what realm of space these ships were launched. Was it ages ago in some actual workshop in an extinct civilisation, and were these but images in the eternal memory? Or were they launched by my own spirit from some magical arsenal of being, and, if so, with what intent? Or were they images of things yet to be in

the world, begotten in that eternal mind
where past, present and future coexist, and
from which they stray into the imagination
of scientist, engineer or poet to be out-realised
in discovery, mechanism or song ?   I find it
impossible to decide.   Sometimes I even
speculate on a world interpenetrating ours
where another sun is glowing, and other stars
are shining over other woods, mountains,
rivers and another race of beings.   And I
know not why it should not be so.   We are
forced into such speculations when we become
certain that no power in us of which we are
conscious is concerned in the creation of such
visionary forms.   If these ships were launched
so marvellously upon the visionary air by
some transcendent artisan of the spirit they
must have been built for some purpose and
for what ?   I was not an engineer intent on
aerial flight, but this is, I think, notable that at
the moment of vision I seemed to myself to
understand the mechanism of these airships,
and I felt, if I could have stepped out of this
century into that visionary barque, I could
have taken the wheel and steered it con-
fidently on to its destiny.   I knew that the
closing of a tube at one side of the bow would
force the ship to steer in that direction,

because the force jetted from the parallel tube on the other side, no longer balanced by an equal emission of power, operated to bring about the change. There is an interest in speculating about this impression of knowledge for it might indicate some complicity of the subconscious mind with the vision which startled the eye. That knowledge may have been poured on the one while seeing was granted to the other. If the vision was imagination, that is if the airship was launched from my own spirit, I must have been in council with the architect, perhaps in deep sleep. If I suppose it was imagination I am justified in trying by every means to reach with full consciousness to the arsenal where such wonders are wrought. I cannot be content to accept it as imagination and not try to meet the architect. As for these visions of airships and for many others I have been unable to place them even speculatively in any world or any century, and it must be so with the imaginations of many other people. But I think that when we begin speculation about these things it is the beginning of our wakening from the dream of life.

I have suggested that images of things to be may come into our sphere out of a being where time does not exist. I have had myself no definite proof as yet that any vision I saw was prophetic, and only one which suggested itself as such to me, and this was so remarkable that I put it on record, because if it was prophetic its significance may become apparent later on. I was meditating about twenty-one years ago in a little room, and my meditation was suddenly broken by a series of pictures which flashed before me with the swiftness of moving pictures in a theatre. They had no relation I could discover to the subject of my meditation, and were interpolated into it then perhaps, because in a tense state of concentration when the brain becomes luminous it is easier to bring to consciousness what has to be brought. I was at the time much more interested in the politics of eternity than in the politics of my own country, and would not have missed an hour of my passionate meditation on the spirit to have witnessed the most dramatic spectacle in any of our national movements. In this meditation I was brought to a wooded valley beyond which was a mountain, and between heaven and earth over the valley was a vast figure aureoled with light, and it descended from that circle of light and assumed human shape, and stood before me and looked at me. The face of this figure was broad and noble in type, beardless and dark-haired. It was in its breadth akin to the face of the young Napoleon, and I would refer both to a common archetype. This being looked at me and vanished, and was instantly replaced by another vision, and this second vision was of a woman with a blue cloak around her shoulders, who came into a room and lifted a young child upon her lap, and from all Ireland rays of light converged on that child. Then this disappeared and was on the instant followed by another picture in the series ; and here I was brought from Ireland to look on the coronation throne at Westminster, and there sat on it a figure of empire which grew weary and let fall the sceptre from its fingers, and itself then drooped and fell and disappeared from the famous seat. And after that in swift succession came another scene, and a gigantic figure, wild and distraught, beating a drum, stalked up and down, and wherever its feet fell there were sparks and the swirling of flame and black smoke upward as from burning cities. It was like the Red Swineherd of legend which beat men into an insane frenzy ;

and when that distraught figure vanished I saw the whole of Ireland lit up from mountain to sea, spreading its rays to the heavens as in the vision which Brigid the seeress saw and told to Patrick. All I could make of that sequence was that some child of destiny, around whom the future of Ireland was to pivot, was born then or to be born, and that it was to be an avatar was symbolised by the descent of the first figure from the sky, and that before that high destiny was to be accomplished the power of empire was to be weakened, and there was to be one more tragic episode in Irish history. Whether this is truth or fantasy time alone can tell. No drums that have since beaten in this land seem to me to be mad enough to be foretold of in that wild drumming. What can I say of such a vision but that it impressed me to forgetfulness of analysis, for what it said was more important than any philosophy of its manner. I have tried to reason over it with myself, as I would with a sequence of another character, to deduce from a sequence better than could be done from a single vision, valid reasons for believing that there must be a conscious intellect somewhere behind the sequence. But I cannot reason

over it. I only know that I look everywhere in the face of youth, in the aspect of
every new notability, hoping before I die to
recognise the broad-browed avatar of my
vision.

HAVE IMAGINATIONS BODY?

In the literature of science I read of marvellously delicate instruments devised to make clear to the intellect the mode of operation of forces invisible to the eye, how Alpha rays, Gamma rays, or the vibrations in metal or plant are measured, and I sigh for some device to aid the intellect in solving difficult problems of psychology. I ask myself how may I ascertain with a precision of knowledge which would convince others whether the figures of vision, imagination or dream are two or three dimensional. The figures cast on the screen in a theatre are on the flat, but have all the illusion of motion, distance, shadow, light and form. The figures of human memory I am content to accept as being in two dimensions. They are imprinted by waves of light on the retina, and cast upon some screen in the brain. But I am forced by my own experience and that of others to believe that nature has a memory, and that it is accessible to us. But this memory cannot be recorded as ours through bodily organs of sight or hearing, nor can imagination make clear to me how any medium could exist in nature which would reflect upon itself as a mirror reflects, or as human vision reflects, an impression intelligible to us of what is passing. If there were such a medium, acting as a mirror to nature or life, and retaining the impression, it must be universal as the supposed æther of the scientist; and how could impressions on this medium intelligible to us be focussed as the vibrations of light are through the needle-point of the eye to record a single view-point? In our visions of the memory of nature we see undistorted figures. If we could imagine the whole body to be sensitive to light, as is that single point in the brain on which the optic nerves converge, what kind of vision would we have? The earth under foot, objects right, left, above and below, would all clamour in various monstrous shapes for attention. The feet would see from one angle, the hands from another, back and front would confuse us; so I cannot imagine the recording power in nature as reflecting like a mirror, and retaining and recording the impressions. But we have another mode of memory in ourselves which might suggest the mode of memory in nature, that by which our subjective life is recorded. Mood, thought, passion, ecstasy, all are preserved for us, can be summoned up and re-created. How is this memory maintained? Are we continuously casting off by way of emanation an image of ourselves instant by instant, infinitesimally delicate but yet complete? Is every motion of mind and body preserved so that a complete facsimile, an effigy in three dimensions, exists of every moment in our being. Is the memory of nature like that? Is it by a continuous emanation of itself it preserves for itself its own history? Does this hypothesis lay too heavy a burden on the substance of the universe as we know it? I do not like to use arguments the validity of which I am not myself able to establish. But I might recall that an eminent thinker in science, Balfour Stewart, supposed of the æther that there was a continual transference of energy to it from the visible universe, and that this stored-up energy might form the basis of an immortal memory for man and nature.

The conception did not lay too heavy a burden on matter as he imagined it. But what is matter ? Is it not pregnant every atom of it with the infinite ? Even in visible nature does not every minutest point of space reflect as a microcosm the macrocosm of earth and heaven ? This minute point of space occupied by my eye as I stand on the mountain has poured into it endless vistas of manifolded mountains, vales, woods, cities, glittering seas, clouds and an infinite blueness. Wherever I move, whether by rays or waves of light, from the farthest star to the nearest leaf with its complexity of vein and tint, there comes to that pin-point of space, the eye, a multitudinous vision. If every pin-point of external space is dense yet not blind with immensity, what more miracle of subtlety, of ethereal delicacy, could be affirmed of matter and be denied because it strains belief ? In that acorn which lies at my feet there is a tiny cell which has in it a memory of the oak from the beginning of earth, and a power coiled in it which can beget from itself the full majestic being of the oak. From that tiny fountain by some miracle can spring another cell, and cell after cell will be born, will go on dividing, begetting, building up from each other unnumbered myriads of cells, all controlled by some mysterious power latent in the first, so that in an hundred years they will, obeying the plan of the tiny architect, have built up "the green-robed senators of mighty woods." There is nothing incredible in the assumption that every cell in the body is wrapped about with myriad memories. He who attributes least mystery to matter is furthest from truth, and he nighest who conjectures the Absolute to be present in fullness of being in the atom. If I am reproached for the supposition that the soul of earth preserves memory of itself by casting off instant by instant enduring images of its multitudinous life, I am only saying of nature in its fullness what visible nature is doing in its own fashion without cessation. What problem of mind, vision, imagination or dream do I solve by this hypothesis? I have been perplexed as an artist by the obedience of the figures of imagination to suggestion from myself. Let me illustrate my perplexity. I imagine a group of white-robed Arabs standing on a sandy hillock and they seem of such a noble dignity that I desire

to paint them. With a restlessness akin
to that which makes a portrait - painter
arrange and rearrange his sitter, until he
gets the pose which satisfies him, I say to
myself, " I wish they would raise their arms
above their heads," and at the suggestion
all the figures in my vision raise their hands
as if in salutation of the dawn.   I see other
figures in imagination which attract me as
compositions.   There may be a figure sitting
down and I think it would compose better
if it was turned in another direction, and
that figure will obey my suggestion, not
always, but at times it will ; and again and
again when I who paint almost entirely from
what is called imagination, and who never
use models, watch a figure in my vision it
will change its motions as I will it.   Now
this is to me amazing.   The invention and
actual drawing of the intricate pattern of
light and shade involved by the lifting of
the hands of my imaginary Arabs would be
considerable.   My brain does not by any
swift action foresee in detail the pictorial
consequences involved by the lifting of arms,
but yet by a single wish, a simple mental
suggestion, the intricate changes are made
in the figures of imagination as they would

be if real Arabs stood before me and raised their hands at my call. If I ask a crowd of people to whom I speak to change their position so that they may the better hear me I am not astonished at the infinite complexity of the change I bring about, because I realise that the will in each one has mastery over the form by some miracle, and the message runs along nerve and muscle, and the simple wish brings about the complex change. But how do I lay hold of the figures in dream or imagination ? By what miracle does the simple wish bring about the complex changes ? It may now be seen why I asked for some means by which I might ascertain whether the forms in dream or imagination are two or three dimensional. If they are on the flat, if they are human memories merely, vibrations of stored-up sunlight fixed in some way in the brain as a photograph is fixed, the alteration of these by a simple wish involves incredibilities. I find Freud, referring to a dream he had, saying carelessly that it was made up by a combination of memories, but yet the architecture of the dream seemed to be coherent and not a patchwork. It had motion of its own. Wonderful, indeed, that the wonder of what was written about so easily was not seen ! How could we imagine even the mightiest conscious artistic intelligence, with seership into all the memories of a life, taking the vibrations which constituted this hand, and adjusting them to the vibrations which made that other arm, or even taking the vibrations which registered a complete figure and amending these so that the figure moved with different gestures from the first gestures recorded as memory ? If such a picture was made up even from life-size images it would be a patchwork and the patches would show everywhere. But the dream figure or the figure of imagination will walk about with authentic motions and undistorted anatomies. Does not the effort to imagine such recombinations even by the mightiest conscious intellect involve incredibilities ? At least it is so with the artist who watches form with a critical eye. How much greater the incredibility if we suppose there was no conscious artist, but that all this authentic imagery of imagination or dream came together without an intelligence to guide it ? But how do we better matters if we assume that the figures in dream or imagination are three dimensional, and that they have actual body and organisation however ethereal, delicate or subtle? If they are shadows or effigies emanated from living organisms, and are complete in their phantasmal nature within and without it is possible to imagine life laying hold of them. It is conceivable that the will may direct their motions even as at a word of command soldiers will turn and march. That is why I suggest that the memory of nature may be by way of emanation or shadow of life and form, and why when we see such images they are not the monstrous complexities they would be if they were reflections on some universal æther spread everywhere taking colour from everything at every possible angle and remaining two dimensional. The hypothesis that everything in nature, every living being, is a continuous fountain of phantasmal effigies of itself would explain the way in which ruins build up their antique life to the eye of the seer, so that he sees the people of a thousand years ago in their cities which are now desolate, and the dark-skinned merchants unrolling their bales in the market, and this is why they appear as some one has said, " thinking the thought and performing the deed." If we have access to such memories, and if they have organism within as well as without, can we not imagine will or desire of ours constraining them? Can we not imagine such forms swept into the vortex of a dreaming soul swayed by the sea of passion in which they exist and acting according to suggestion? And if we suppose that a deeper being of ours has wider vision than the waking consciousness, and can use the memories, not only of this plane of being, but of the forms peculiar to mid-world and heaven-world, this might help to solve some of the perplexities aroused in those who are intent and vigilant observers of their own dreams and imaginations. Continually in my analysis of the figures I see I am forced to follow them beyond the transitory life I know and to speculate upon the being of the Ever Living. I think there is no half-way house between the spiritual and the material where the intellect can dwell; and if we find we have our being in a universal life we must alter our values, change all our ideas until they depend upon and are in harmony with that sole cause of all that is.

INTUITION

THAT sense of a divinity ever present in act or thought my words do not communicate. The ecstatic, half-articulate, with broken words, can make us feel the kingdom of heaven is within him. I choose words with reverence but speak from recollection, and one day does not utter to another its own wisdom. Our highest moments in life are often those of which we hold thereafter the vaguest memories. We may have a momentary illumination yet retain almost as little of its reality as ocean keeps the track of a great vessel which went over its waters. I remember incidents rather than moods, vision more than ecstasy. How can I now, passed away from myself and long at other labours, speak of what I felt in those years when thought was turned to the spirit, and no duty had as yet constrained me to equal outward effort? I came to feel akin to

those ancestors of the Aryan in remote
spiritual dawns when Earth first extended
its consciousness into humanity. In that
primal ecstasy and golden age was born that
grand spiritual tradition which still remains
embodied in Veda and Upanishad, in Persian
and Egyptian myth, and which trails glimmering with colour and romance over our own
Celtic legends. I had but a faint glow of that
which to the ancestors was full light. I
could not enter that Radiance they entered
yet Earth seemed to me bathed in an aether
of Deity. I felt at times as one raised from
the dead, made virginal and pure, who
renews exquisite intimacies with the divine
companions, with Earth, Water, Air and
Fire. To breathe was to inhale magical
elixirs. To touch Earth was to feel the
influx of power as with one who had touched
the mantle of the Lord. Thought, from
whatever it set out, for ever led to the
heavenly city. But these feelings are in-
communicable. We have no words to express a thousand distinctions clear to the
spiritual sense. If I tell of my exaltation
to another, who has not felt this himself,
it is explicable to that person as the joy
in perfect health, and he translates into

lower terms what is the speech of the gods to men.

I began writing desirous to picture things definitely to the intellect and to speak only of that over which there could be reason and argument, but I have often been indefinite as when I said in an earlier chapter that earth seemed an utterance of gods, "Every flower was a thought. The trees were speech. The grass was speech. The winds were speech. The waters were speech." But what does that convey ? Many feel ecstasy at the sight of beautiful natural objects, and it might be said it does not interpret emotion precisely to make a facile reference to a divine world. I believe of nature that it is a manifestation of Deity, and that, because we are partakers in the divine nature, all we see has affinity with us ; and though now we are as children who look upon letters before they have learned to read, to the illuminated spirit its own being is clearly manifested in the universe even as I recognise my thought in the words I write. Everything in nature has intellectual significance, and relation as utterance to the Thought out of which the universe was born, and we, whose minds were made in its image, who are the microcosm of the macrocosm, have in ourselves the key to unlock the meaning of that utterance. Because of these affinities the spirit swiftly by intuition can interpret nature to itself even as our humanity instinctively comprehends the character betrayed by the curve of lips or the mood which lurks within haunting eyes. We react in numberless ways to that myriad nature about us and within us, but we retain for ourselves the secret of our response, and for lack of words speak to others of these things only in generalities. I desire to be precise, and having searched memory for some instance of that divine speech made intelligible to myself which I could translate into words which might make it intelligible to others, I recollected something which may at least be understood if not accepted. It was the alphabet of the language of the gods.

This was a definite exercise of intuition undertaken in order to evolve intellectual order out of a chaos of impressions and to discover the innate affinities of sound with idea, element, force, colour and form. I found as the inner being developed it used a symbolism of its own. Sounds, forms and colours, which had an established significance in the complicated artifice of our external intercourse with each other, took on new meanings in the spirit as if it spoke a language of its own and wished to impart it to the infant Psyche. If these new meanings did not gradually reveal an intellectual character, to pursue this meditation, to encourage the association of new ideas with old symbols would be to encourage madness. Indeed the partial uprising of such ideas, the fact that a person associates a vowel with a certain colour or a colour with a definite emotion is regarded by some as indicating incomplete sanity. I tried to light the candle on my forehead to peer into every darkness in the belief that the external universe of nature had no more exquisite architecture than the internal universe of being, and that the light could only reveal some lordlier chambers of the soul, and whatever speech the inhabitant used must be fitting for its own sphere, so I became a pupil of the spirit and tried as a child to learn the alphabet at the knees of the gods.

I was led first to brood upon the elements of human speech by that whisper of the word "Aeon" out of the darkness, for among the many thoughts I had at the time came the thought that speech may originally have been

intuitive. I discarded the idea with regard
to that word, but the general speculation
remained with me, and I recurred to it again
and again, and began brooding upon the
significance of separate letters, and had related
many letters to abstractions or elements, when
once again, seemingly by chance, I took down
a book from a shelf. It was a volume of
the Upanishads, and it opened at a page
where my eye caught this : "From that Self
came the air, from air fire, from fire water,
from water earth." I quote from a distant
memory but the words are, I think, close
enough. What excited me was that I had
already discovered what I thought were the
sound equivalents for the self, motion, fire,
water and earth ; and the order of the cosmic
evolution of the elements suggested in the
passage quoted led me to consider whether
there was any intellectual sequence in the
human sound equivalents of elements and
ideas. I then began to rearrange the roots
of speech in their natural order from throat
sounds, through dental to labials, from A
which begins to be recognisable in the throat
to M in the utterance of which the lips
are closed. An intellectual sequence of ideas
became apparent. This encouraged me to

try and complete the correspondences arrived at intuitively. I was never able to do this. Several sounds failed, however I brooded upon them, to suggest their intellectual affinities, and I can only detail my partial discoveries and indicate where harmonies may be found between my own intuitions about language and the roots of speech and in what primitive literature are intuitions akin to my own.

In trying to arrive at the affinities of sound with thought I took letter after letter, brooding upon them, murmuring them again and again, and watching intensely every sensation in consciousness, every colour, form or idea which seemed evoked by the utterance. No doubt the sanity of the boy who walked about the roads at night more than thirty years ago murmuring letters to himself with the reverence of a mystic murmuring the Ineffable Name might have been questioned by any one who knew that he was trying to put himself in the place of his Aryan ancestors, and to find as they might have found the original names for earth, air, water, fire, the forces and elements of the nature which was all about them. Even as in the myth in Genesis beings were named by the earliest man, so I invited

the Heavenly Man to renew for me that first
speech, and to name the elements as they
were by those who looked up at the sky, and
cried out the name of the fire in the sky
from a God-given intuition.

THE LANGUAGE OF THE GODS

If I interpreted rightly that dweller in the mind, the true roots of human speech are vowels and consonants, each with affinity to idea, force, colour and form, the veriest abstractions of these, but by their union into words expressing more complex notions, as atoms and molecules by their union form the compounds of the chemist. It is difficult to discover single words of abstract significance to represent adequately the ideas associated with these rudiments of speech. Every root is charged with significance, being the symbol of a force which is itself the fountain of many energies, even as primordial being when manifested rolls itself out into numberless forms, states of energy and consciousness. The roots of human speech are the sound correspondences of powers which in their combination and interaction make up the universe. The mind of man is made in the image of Deity, and the elements of speech are related to the powers in his mind and through it to the being of the Oversoul.

These true roots of language are few, alphabet and roots being identical. The first root is A, the sound symbol for the self in man and Deity in the cosmos. Its form equivalent is the circle ◯. The second root is R, representing motion. Its colour correspondence is red, and its form symbol is the line |.

Motion engenders heat, and the third root following the order from throat sounds to labials is H, the sound correspondence of Heat. Its symbol is the triangle △, and it has affinity with the colour orange.

Motion and heat are the begetters of Fire, the sound equivalent of which is the root L, which in form is symbolised by lines radiating from a point as in this figure 人. L is fire, light or radiation, and it is followed in the series of roots by Y which symbolises the reaction in nature against that radiation of energy. It is the sound equivalent of binding, concentration or condensation. Matter in the cosmos is obeying the law of gravitation and gathering into fire-mists preliminary to its knotting into suns and planets. The colour affinity is yellow. In man it is will which focuses energy and concentrates it to a burning-point for the accomplishing of desire. Its form symbol is ♈ representing a vortex or spiral movement inward, opposing in this the expansion or radiation implied in the root L.

The root which follows Y is W, the sound symbol of liquidity or water. Its form is semilunar, ◡, and I think its colour is green.

We have now descended to earth and with this descent comes dualism, and henceforth all the roots have companion roots. Primordial substance has lost its ethereal character and has settled into a solid or static condition. The two roots which express this are G and K ; G is the symbol of earth, as K is of mineral, rock, crystal or hardness of any kind. I could discover with no certainty any colour affinities for either of these roots, and about the forms I am also uncertain though I was moved to relate G with the square ☐ and K with the square crossed by a diagonal ◈.

The twin roots next in the series are S and Z, and I can find no better words to indicate the significance of the first than impregnation, inbreathing or insouling. We have reached in evolution the stage when the one life breaks into myriads of lives, which on earth finds its correspondence in the genesis of the cell. Z represents the multiplication, division or begetting of organism from organism. It is the out-breathing or bringing to birth of the seed which is sown. The form symbol of S is, I think, Θ, and of Z ⊕. I discovered no colour affinities for either.

The duality of roots succeeding this is TH and SH. The first is the sound equivalent of growth, expansion or swelling, and its twin root represents that state where the limit of growth in a particular form is reached and a scattering or dissolution of its elements takes place. In the vegetable world we might find an illustration in the growth and decay of a plant.

After these twain come the duality of T and D. I found great difficulty in discovering words to express the abstractions related to these. Yet in meditating on them with reference to the T, I was continually haunted by the idea of individual action, movement or initiative, and I believe it refers to that state when life divorced from its old interior unity with the source of life, and, confined in a form, begins in its imagination of itself to be an ego, is in a state of outgoing, acts and looks outward, touches and tastes ; while D represents the reverse side of that, its reaction or absorption inward to silence, sleep, immobility, abeyance.   The form symbol T is + and ⌓ vaguely suggested itself to me as the symbol of D.

There is a parallelism between T and TH as there is between D and SH, T representing movement of the thing by itself while TH represents growth or expansion merely, while D represents the more subjective sinking of a thing into abeyance of its powers as SH represents the external resolving of an organism into its elements.

For the dualism of roots J and TCH my intuition failed utterly to discover correlations, and when I had placed the roots in their correct sequence and endeavoured by intellect and reason to arrive at the logical significance these two might have in the series of sounds, I could never satisfy myself that I had come nigh to any true affinity, so I pass these by.

The roots which follow are V and F, of which the first refers to life in water, to all that swims, while F is related to what lives in air and flies. I am doubtful about the form symbols, but colour affinities began here again, and blue suggested itself to me as the correspondence, while the twin roots which come after them, P and B, are related to indigo, the dark blue.

Life has now reached the human stage, is divided into sexes, and P is the sound symbol for life masculine or paternity, while B represents feminine life or maternity.

The series closes with N and M. The first of these represents continuance of being, immortality if you will, while the last root, in the utterance of which the lips are closed, has the sense of finality, it is the close, limit, measure, end or death of things. Their colour affinities are with violet. In all there are twenty-one consonants which with the vowels make up the divine roots of speech.

The vowels are the sound symbols of consciousness in seven moods or states, while the consonants represent states of matter and modes of energy.

I despair of any attempt to differentiate from each other the seven states of consciousness represented by the vowels. How

shall I make clear the difference between
A where consciousness in man or cosmos
begins manifestation, utterance or limitation of itself, and OO where consciousness
is returning into itself, breaking from the
limitation of form and becoming limitless
once more ; or E when it has become
passional, or I where it has become egoistic,
actively intellectual or reasoning, or O where
it has become intuitional.   Our psychology
gives me no names for these states, but the
vowel root always represents consciousness,
and, in its union with the consonant root,
modifies or defines its significance, doing
that again as it precedes or follows it.   I
once held more completely than I do now
an interior apprehension of the significance
of all, and I might perhaps, if I had con-
centrated more intently, have completed
more fully the correspondences with idea,
colour and form.   But life attracts us in
too many ways, and when I was young
and most sensitive and intuitional I did
not realise the importance of what I was
attempting to do.

This so far as I know is the only considered effort made by any one to ascertain
the value of intuition as a faculty by using

it in reference to matters where the intellect was useless but where the results attained by intuition could be judged by the reason. Intuition is a faculty of which many speak with veneration, but it seems rarely to be evoked consciously, and, if it is witness to a knower in man, it surely needs testing and use like any other faculty. I have exercised intuition with respect to many other matters and with inward conviction of the certainty of truth arrived at in this way, but they were matters relating to consciousness and were not by their nature easily subject to ratification by the reason. These intuitions in respect of language are to some extent capable of being reasoned or argued over, and I submit them for consideration by others whose study of the literature, learning and language of the ancients may give them special authority.

ANCIENT INTUITIONS

EVEN where I had a certitude that my attribution of element, form or colour to a root was right I have never thought this exhausted the range of its affinities in our manifold being. I went but a little way within myself, but felt that greater powers awaited discovery within us, powers whose shadowy skirts flicker on the surface of consciousness but with motion so impalpable that we leave them nameless. The root I relate to light may have correspondence also with another power which is to the dark divinity of being what light is to the visible world. I have never thought that the languages spoken by men had all their origin in one intuitional speech. There may have been many beginnings in that undiscoverable antiquity. But I believe that one, or perhaps several, among the early races, more spiritual than the rest,

was prompted by intuition, while others
may have developed speech in any of the
ways suggested by biologists and scholars.
The genius of some races leads them to
seek for light within as the genius of others
leads them to go outward. I imagine a
group of the ancestors lit up from within,
endowed with the primal blessings of youth
and ecstasy, the strings of their being not
frayed as ours are, nor their God-endowed
faculties abused, still exquisitely sensitive,
feeling those kinships and affinities with the
elements which are revealed in the sacred
literature of the Aryan, and naming these
affinities from an impulse springing up within.
I can imagine the spirit struggling outwards
making of element, colour, form or sound a
mirror, on which, outside itself, it would
find symbols of all that was pent within itself,
and so gradually becoming self-conscious in
the material nature in which it was embodied,
but which was still effigy or shadow of a
divine original. I can imagine them looking
up at the fire in the sky, and calling out " El "
if it was the light they adored, or if they
rejoiced in the heat and light together they
would name it " Hel."   Or if they saw death,
and felt it as the stillness or ending of motion

or breath, they would say " Mor." Or if
the fire acting on the water made it boil,
they would instinctively combine the sound
equivalents of water and fire, and " Wal "
would be the symbol. If the fire of life was
kindled in the body to generate its kind, the
sound symbol would be " Lub." When the
axe was used to cut, its hardness would
prompt the use of the hard or metallic affinity
in sound, and " Ak " would be to cut or
pierce. One extension of meaning after
another would rapidly increase the wealth of
significance, and recombinations of roots the
power of expression. The root " M " with
its sense of finality would suggest " Mi " to
diminish, and as to measure a thing is to go
to its ends, " Ma " would also mean to measure,
and as to think a thing is to measure it,
" Ma " would also come to be associated
with thinking. I had nearly all my correspondences vividly in mind before I inquired
of friends more learned than myself what
were the reputed origins of human speech,
and in what books I could find whatever
knowledge there was, and then I came upon
the Aryan roots ; and there I thought and
still think are to be found many evidences in
corroboration of my intuitions. There are

pitfalls for one who has no pretensions to
scholarship in tracking words to their origins,
and it is a labour for the future in conjunction with one more learned than myself to
elucidate these intuitions in regard to the
roots, and to go more fully into the psychology which led to rapid extension of meanings until words were created, which at first
sight seem to have no relation to the root
values. I still believe I can see in the Aryan
roots an intelligence struggling outward
from itself to recognise its own affinities in
sound. But I wish here only to give indica-
tions and directions of approach to that
Divine Mind whose signature is upon us
in everything, and whose whole majesty is
present in the least thing in nature. I have
written enough to enable those who are
curious to exercise their intuitions or
analytic faculty in conjunction with their
scholarship, to test the worth of my intuitions. Intuition must be used in these
correspondences, for the art of using them is
not altogether discoverable by the intellect.
I hope also that my partial illumination will
be completed, corrected or verified by others.

A second line of investigation I suggest is
the study of some harmony of primitive

alphabets, such as that compiled by Forster, and, after arranging the letters in their natural order from throat sounds to labials, to see if there is not much to lead us to suppose that there was an original alphabet, where the form equivalents of sound proceeded in an orderly way from the circle through the line, the triangle and the other forms I have indicated. Perhaps the true correspondences were retained as an esoteric secret by the wisest, because there may have been in them the key to mysteries only to be entrusted to those many times tested before the secret of the use of power was disclosed. And again I would suggest a study of that science of divine correspondences which is embodied in mystical Indian literature. The correspondences of form, colour or force with letters given there are not always in agreement with my own. Sometimes as in the Bagavadgita where Krishna, the Self of the Manifested Universe, says, " I am the A among letters," I find agreement. In other works like the Shivagama there is partial agreement as where it says, " Meditate upon the fire force with R as its symbol, as being triangular and red." The colour and the letter are here in harmony with my own intuitions, but the form is not, and I am more inclined to believe my own intuition to be true because I find in so many of the primitive alphabets the form symbol of R is the line coming out of a circle. The water force is given in the same book a semilunar form as correspondence, but its sound symbol is given as V and not W. The earth force is given as quadrangular in form as I imagine it, but the colour is yellow. I have not investigated the consonants in their attribution to the nervous system given in such books. I have no doubt that in a remoter antiquity the roots of language were regarded as sacred, and when chanted every letter was supposed to stir into motion or evoke some subtle force in the body. Tone and word combined we know will thrill the nervous system, and this is specially so with lovers of music and persons whose virgin sensitiveness of feeling has never been blunted by excess. A word chanted or sung will start the wild fires leaping in the body, like hounds which hear their master calling them by name, and to those whose aspiration heavenward has purified their being there comes at last a moment when at the calling of the Ineffable Name the Holy Breath rises as a flame and the shadow man goes forth to become one with the ancestral self.

What is obvious in that ancient literature is the belief in a complete circle of correspondences between every root sound in the human voice and elements, forms and colours, and that the alphabet was sacred in character. Intuitions which modern psychologists regard as evidence of decadence are found present in the literature of antiquity. The attributions sometimes are the same as mine ; sometimes they differ, but they suggest the same theory of a harmony of microcosm with macrocosm, and it is carried out so that every centre in the body is named by the name of a divine power. It is only by a spiritual science we can recover identity, renew and make conscious these affinities. Life had other labours for me from which I could not escape, and I had not for long the leisure in which to reknit the ties between myself and the ancestral being. But while I still had leisure I experienced those meltings of the external into intelligible meanings. The form of a flower long brooded upon would translate itself into energies, and these would resolve themselves finally into states of consciousness, intelligible to me while I experienced them, but too

remote from the normal for words to tell
their story.   I may have strayed for a moment
into that Garden of the Divine Mind where,
as it is said in Genesis, "He made every
flower before it was in the field and every
herb before it grew."   My failure to find
words to express what I experienced made
me concentrate more intensely upon the
relation of form and colour to consciousness
in the hope that analysis might make intellectual exposition possible.   I do not wish
to linger too long on the analysis I made.
The message of nature is more important than
the symbols used to convey it, and, in de-
tailing these correspondences, I feel rather as
one who reading Shelley's "Hymn of Pan"
ignored all that ecstasy and spoke merely of
spelling or verse structure.   But why do I
say that ?   The works of the Magician of the
Beautiful are not like ours and in the least
fragment His artistry is no less present than
in the stars.   We may enter the infinite
through the minute no less than through
contemplation of the vast.   I thought in that
early ecstasy of mine when I found how near
to us was the King in His Beauty that I could
learn to read that marvellous writing on the
screen of Nature and teach it to others ; and,

as a child first learns its letters with difficulty, but after a time leaps to the understanding of their combination, and later, without care for letters or words, follows out the thought alone ; so I thought the letters of the divine utterance might be taught and the spirit in man would leap by intuition to the thought of the Spirit making that utterance.   For all that vast ambition I have not even a complete alphabet to show, much less one single illustration of how to read the letters of nature in their myriad intricacies of form, colour and sound in the world we live in. But I believe that vision has been attained by the seers, and we shall all at some time attain it, and, as is said in the Divine Shepherd of Hermes, it shall meet us everywhere, plain and easy, walking or resting, waking or sleeping, "for there is nothing which is not the image of God."

POWER

I HAVE spoken of a training of the will, but have not indicated the spring of power in our being, nor dilated on those moments when we feel a Titanic energy lurks within us ready to our summons as the familiar spirit to the call of the enchanter. If we have not power we are nothing and must remain outcasts of the Heavens. We must be perfect as the Father is perfect. If in the being of the Ancient of Days there is power, as there is wisdom and beauty, we must liken ourselves to that being, partake, as our nature will permit, of its power, or we can never enter it. The Kingdom is taken by violence. The easier life becomes in our civilisations, the remoter we are from nature, the more does power ebb away from most of us. It ebbs away for all but those who never relax the will but sustain it hour by hour. We even grow to dread the powerful person because

we feel how phantasmal before power are
beauty and wisdom, and indeed there is no
true beauty or wisdom which is not allied
with strength.   For one who cultivates will
in himself there are thousands who cultivate
the intellect or follow after beauty, and that
is because the intellect can walk easily on the
level places, while at first every exercise of
the will is laborious as the lift is to the climber
of a precipice.   Few are those who come to
that fullness of power where the will becomes
a fountain within them perpetually springing
up self-fed, and who feel like the mountain
lovers who know that it is easier to tread on
the hilltops than to walk on the low and level
roads.   Because in our ordered life power
is continually ebbing away from us, nature,
which abhors a vacuum in our being, is
perpetually breaking up our civilisations by
wars or internal conflicts, so that stripped of
our ease, in battle, through struggle and
sacrifice, we may grow into power again ;
and this must continue until we tread the
royal road, and cultivate power in our being
as we cultivate beauty or intellect.   Those
who have in themselves the highest power,
who are miracle-workers, the Buddhas and
the Christs, are also the teachers of peace,

and they may well be so having themselves attained mastery of the Fire.

It is because it is so laborious to cultivate the will we find in literature endless analysis of passion and thought, but rarely do we find one writing as if he felt the powers leaping up in his body as the thronged thoughts leap up in the brain. I was never able to recognise that harmony of powers spoken of by the ancients as inhabiting the house of the body, lurking in nerve-centre or plexus, or distinguish their functions, but I began to feel, after long efforts at concentration and mastery of the will, the beginning of an awakening of the fires, and at times there came partial perception of the relation of these forces to centres in the psychic body. I could feel them in myself; and sometimes see them, or the vibration or light of them, about others who were seekers with myself for this knowledge; so that the body of a powerful person would appear to be throwing out light in radiation from head or heart, or plumes of fire would rise above the head jetting from fountains within, apparitions like wings of fire, plumes or feathers of flame, or dragon-like crests, many-coloured. Once at the apex of intensest meditation I awoke that fire in myself of which the ancients have written, and it ran up like lightning along the spinal cord, and my body rocked with the power of it, and I seemed to myself to be standing in a fountain of flame, and there were fiery pulsations as of wings about my head, and a musical sound not unlike the clashing of cymbals with every pulsation ; and if I had remembered the ancient wisdom I might have opened that eye which searches infinitude. But I remembered only, in a half terror of the power I had awakened, the danger of misdirection of the energy, for such was the sensation of power that I seemed to myself to have opened the seal of a cosmic fountain, so I remained contemplative and was not the resolute guider of the fire. And indeed this rousing of the fire is full of peril ; and woe to him who awakens it before he has purified his being into selflessness, for it will turn downward and vitalise his darker passions and awaken strange frenzies and inextinguishable desires. The turning earthward of that heaven-born power is the sin against the Holy Breath, for that fire which leaps upon us in the ecstasy of contemplation of Deity is the Holy Breath, the power which can

carry us from Earth to Heaven. It is
normally known to man only in procreation,
but its higher and mightier uses are unknown
to him. Even though in our scriptures it
is said of it that it gives to this man vision
or the discerning of spirits, and to that
poetry or eloquence, and to another healing
and magical powers, it remains for most a
myth of the theologians, and is not mentioned
by any of our psychologists though it is the
fountain out of which is born all other
powers in the body and is the sustainer of
all our faculties. Normally I found this
power in myself, not leaping up Titanically
as if it would storm the heavens, but a steady
light in the brain, "the candle upon the
forehead," and it was revealed in ecstasy of
thought or power in speech, and in a continuous welling up from within myself of
intellectual energy, vision or imagination.
It is the afflatus of the poet or musician.
As an ancient scripture says of it, "The
Illuminator is the inspirer of the poet, the
jeweller, the chiseller and all who work in
the arts." It is the Promethean fire, and
only by mastery of this power will man be
able to ascend to the ancestral Paradise.
Again and again I would warn all who read

of the danger of awakening it, and again and
again I would say that without this power
we are as nothing. We shall never scale the
Heavens, and religions, be they ever so holy,
will never open the gates to us, unless we
are able mightily to open them for ourselves
and enter as the strong spirit who cannot
be denied. This power might cry of itself
to us :

My kinsmen are they, beauty, wisdom, love ;
But without me are none may dare to climb
To the Ancestral Light that glows above
        Its mirrored lights in Time.

King have I been and foe in ages past.
None may escape me. I am foe until
There shall be for the spirit forged at last
        The high unshakable will.

Fear, I will rend you. Love, I make you strong.
Wed with my might the beautiful and wise.
We shall go forth at last, a Titan throng,
        To storm His Paradise.

THE MEMORY OF THE SPIRIT

Hy Brazil, Ildathach, the lands of Immortal Youth which flush with magic the dreams of childhood, for most sink soon below far horizons and do not again arise. For around childhood gather the wizards of the darkness and they baptize it and change its imagination of itself as in the Arabian tales of enchantment men were changed by sorcerers who cried, " Be thou beast or bird." So by the black art of education is the imagination of life about itself changed, and one will think he is a worm in the sight of Heaven, he who is but a god in exile, and another of the Children of the King will believe that he is the offspring of animals. What palaces they were born in, what dominions they are rightly heir to, are concealed from them as in the fairy tale the stolen prince lives obscurely among the swineherds. Yet at times men do not

143

remember, in dream and in the deeps of sleep, they still wear sceptre and diadem and partake of the banquet of the gods. The gods are still living. They are our brothers. They await us. They beckon us to come up to them and sit upon equal thrones. To those who cry out against romance I would say, You yourself are romance. You are the lost prince herding obscurely among the swine. The romance of your spirit is the most marvellous of stories. Your wanderings have been greater than those of Ulysses. You have been Bird of Paradise and free of immensity, and you have been outcast and wingless, huddled under the rocks and despairing of the Heavens. If you will but awaken the inner sight, Hy Brazil, Ildathach, all the lands of Immortal Youth will build themselves up anew for you no longer as fantasy but in vivid actuality. Earth will become magical and sweet as ever. You will be drunken with beauty. You may see the fiery eyes of the Cyclops wandering over the mountains and hear the Bell Branch shaken, the sound that summons the spirit home. From long pondering I have come to believe in the eternity of the spirit and that it is an inhabitant of many spheres, for

I know not how otherwise I can interpret to myself the myriad images that as memories or imaginations cling to it, following it into the body as birds follow the leader in the migratory flock. Looking back on that other life which began to dominate this there are a thousand things I cannot understand except I believe that for myself and for all of us there has been an eternity of being and that many spheres are open to us. If these images are not earth-born, from what land, Elfland, Heaven-world or God-world, do they come ? I have chosen but a few images out of many to explain why I think our dreams and visions come often in all completeness into our sphere out of other spheres of being and are not built up from memories of earth. Looking back upon that other life through the vistas of memory I see breaking in upon the images of this world forms of I know not what antiquity. I walk out of strange cities steeped in the jewel glow and gloom of evening, or sail in galleys over the silvery waves of the antique ocean. I reside in tents, or in palace chambers, go abroad in chariots, meditate in cyclopean buildings, am worshipper of the Earth gods upon the mountains, lie tranced in Egyptian crypts, or brush with naked body through the long sunlit grasses of the prairies.   Endlessly the procession of varying forms goes back into remote yesterdays of the world. How do these self-conceptions spring up ? How are they clothed with the state of ancient civilisations ?   If when I perceived them they were the newest things in the world, and the images were minted that instant by the imagination, out of what treasury of design came the fitting scenery, the always varied buildings, garments and setting of wood, plain or mountain ?   Are they not rather, I ask myself, memories of the spirit incarnated many times ?   And if so, again I ask myself is it only on earth there has been this long ancestry of self ?   For there is another self in me which seemed to know not the world but revealed itself to the listening bodily life in cosmic myths, in remote legends of the Children of Darkness and the Children of Light, and of the revolt against heaven.   And another self seemed to bring with it vision or memory of elemental beings, the shining creatures of water and wood, or who break out in opalescent colour from the rocks or hold their court beneath the ponderous hills.   And there was another self which was akin to the gloomy world of the shades, but recoiled shuddering from them. And there was yet another self which sought out after wisdom, and all these other selves and their wisdom and memories were but tributary to it. The gates of sleep too were often thronged with fleeting presences as I sank into unconsciousness, or was outcast from that innermost being when waking, and I saw but for an instant back into the profundity, and at times it appeared to the imagination as the gate of Eden :

With dreadful faces thronged and fiery arms.

Out of what sphere came that being taller and mightier than human, whose body seemed wrought out of flame and whose eyes had the stillness of an immortal, and who seemed to gaze at me out of eternity as I waked in the night. It was so lofty and above humanity that I seemed to myself to be less than an insect, though something in me cried out to it in brotherhood, and I knew not whether I had fallen from its height, or was a lost comrade lagging far behind in time who should have been equal and companion but was too feeble to rise to such majesty. I know that I have not been alone

in such imaginations for there are few whose
intent will has tried to scale the Heavens
who have not been met by messages from
the gods who are the fountains of this
shadowy beauty, and who are, I think, ourselves beyond this mirage of time and space
by which we are enchanted.   I have spoken
to others, seekers like myself upon this
quest, and recognise identity of vision and
experience.   But I have not been able to
devote to every mental image the thought
which might make its meaning or origin
intelligible.   We cannot do that for the
forms we see move continuously in visible
nature, for we pass them by thinking intensely
but of a few of them.   But our psychology
must take account of every experience of the
soul.   I have not found in latter-day philosophical writers the explanation of my own
experiences, and I think that is because there
has been an over-development of intellect
and few have cultivated vision, and without
that we have not got the first data for fruit-
ful speculation.   We rarely find philosophical
writers referring to vision of their own,
yet we take them as guides on our mental
travelling, though in this world we all would
prefer to have knowledge of earth and

heaven through the eyes of a child rather than to know them only through the musings of one who was blind, even though his intellect was mighty as Kant's.

It is only when I turn to the literature of vision and intuition, to the sacred books and to half sacred tradition, to the poets and seers, that I find a grandiose conception of nature in which every spiritual experience is provided for. I have not entered the paradises they entered but what little I know finds its place in the universe of their vision. Whether they are Syrian, Greek, Egyptian or Hindu, the writers of the sacred books seem to me as men who had all gazed upon the same august vision and reported of the same divinity. Even in our own Gaelic wonder tales I often find a vision which is, I think, authentic, and we can, I believe, learn from these voyages to the Heaven-world more of the geography of the spirit and the many mansions in the being of the Father than we can from the greatest of our sightless philosophers. The Earth-world, Mid-world, Heaven-world and God-world spoken of in the Indian scriptures are worlds our Gaelic ancestors had also knowledge of. When Cormac enters the Heaven-world and is told by those who inhabit it,

" Whenever we imagine the fields to be sown they are sown. Whenever we imagine the fields to be reaped they are reaped," he saw the same world as the seer who wrote in the marvellous Upanishad : " There are no chariots there or roads for chariots. The soul makes for itself chariots and roads for chariots. There are no joys or rejoicings there. The soul makes for itself joys and rejoicings. For the spirit of man is creator." The visionaries of the future will finally justify the visionaries of the past. I do not feel that my knowledge is great enough to do this, nor have I been able to steal from a life made busy by other labours enough time or enough thought even to use in the best way the little I know. I would like to vindicate my predecessors in Ireland and correlate my own vision and the vision of my friends with the vision of those who went before us, for I think when we discard the past and its vision we are like men who, half-way up a mountain, decide foolishly to attempt the ascent from another side of the hill and so continually lose the height which was gained. Our Gaelic ancestors had the gift of seership, and I had thought at one time to reconstruct from the ancient literature the vision of the universe

they had, a labour which might be done by
any who had vision of his own and who was
versed in the comparative study of the religions
of the past, and so make intelligible to those
who live here to-day the thought of their
forefathers, and enable them to begin anew
the meditation towards divine things so often
broken up in our unhappy history. All
literature tends to produce a sacred book by
an evolution of thought of the highest minds
building one upon another. A literature
so continually imaginative, visionary and
beautiful as the Gaelic would, I do not doubt,
have culminated in some magnificent expression of the spirit if life had not been
drawn from central depths to surfaces by
continuous invasions. I think that meditation
is beginning anew, and the powers which
were present to the ancestors are establishing
again their dominion over the spirit. To
some there come startling flashes of vision,
and others feel a hand of power touching
them thrust out from a hidden world.
Whether they know it or not they are the
servants of gods who speak or act through
them and make them the messengers of their
will. I have written down some of my own
thoughts and experiences that others may be

encouraged to believe that by imagination they can lay hold of truth ; and as something must be written about the geography of the spirit by way of guidance to those who rise within themselves in meditation I will try briefly to reconstruct the Celtic vision of Heaven and Earth as I believe it was known to the Druids and bardic seers. Let no one who requires authority read what I have written for I will give none. If the spirit of the reader does not bear witness to truth he will not be convinced even though a Whitley Stokes rose up to verify the written word. Let it be accepted by others as a romantic invention or attribution of divine powers to certain names to make more coherent the confusion of Celtic myth.

CELTIC COSMOGONY

In the beginning was the boundless Lir, an infinite depth, an invisible divinity, neither dark nor light, in whom were all things past and to be. There at the close of a divine day, time being ended, and the Nuts of Knowledge harvested, the gods partake of the Feast of Age and drink from a secret fountain. Their being there is neither life nor death nor sleep nor dream, but all are wondrously wrought together. They lie in the bosom of Lir, cradled in the same peace, those who hereafter shall meet in love or war in hate. The Great Father and the Mother of the Gods mingle together and Heaven and Earth are lost, being one in the Infinite Lir.

Of Lir but little may be affirmed, and nothing can be revealed. In trance alone the seer might divine beyond his ultimate vision this being. It is a breath with many voices which cannot speak in one tone, but utters itself through multitudes.   It is beyond the gods and if they were to reveal it, it could only be through their own departure and a return to the primeval silences.   But in this is the root of existence from which springs the sacred Hazel whose branches are the gods : and as the mystic night trembles into dawn, its leaves and its blossoms and its starry fruit burgeon simultaneously and are shed over the waters of space.   An image of futurity has arisen in the divine imagination : and Sinan, who is also Dana, the Great Mother and Spirit of Nature, grows thirsty to receive its imprint on her bosom, and to bear again her offspring of stars and starry beings.   Then the first fountain is opened and seven streams issue like seven fiery whirlwinds, and Sinan is carried away and mingled with the torrent, and when the force of the torrent is broken, Sinan also meets death.

What other names Connla's Well and the Sacred Hazel have in Celtic tradition may be discovered later, but here, without reference to names, which only bewilder until their significance is made known, it is better to explain with less of symbol this Celtic Cosmogenesis.

We have first of all Lir, an infinite being, neither spirit nor energy nor substance, but rather the spiritual form of these, in which all the divine powers, raised above themselves, exist in a mystic union or trance. This is the night of the gods from which Mananan first awakens, the most spiritual divinity known to the ancient Gael, being the Gaelic equivalent of that Spirit which breathed on the face of the waters. He is the root of existence from which springs the Sacred Hazel, the symbol of life ramifying everywhere : and the forms of this life are conceived first by Mananan, the divine imagination. It throws itself into seven forms or divinities, the branches of the Hazel ; and these again break out endlessly into leaves and blossoms and fruit, into myriads of divine beings, the archetypes and ancestral begetters of those spirits who are the Children of Lir. All these are first in the Divine Darkness and are unrevealed, and Mananan is still the unuttered Word, and is in that state the Chaldaic oracle of Proclus saith of the Divine Mind : "It had not yet gone forth, but abode in the Paternal Depth, and in the adytum of god - nourished Silence."

But Mananan, while one in essence with
the Paternal Lir, is yet, as the divine
imagination, a separate being to whom,
thus brooding, Lir seems apart, or covered
over with a veil, and this aspect of Lir, a
mirage which begins to cover over true
being, is Dana, the Hibernian Mother of
the Gods, or Sinan in the antique Dinn-
shenchus, deity first viewed externally, and
therefore seeming to partake of the nature
of substance, and, as the primal form of
matter, the Spirit of Nature.   Mananan
alone of all the gods exists in the inner side
of this spirit, and therefore it is called his
mantle, which, flung over man or god,
wraps them from the gaze of embodied
beings.   His mantle, the Faed Fia, has
many equivalents in other mythologies.   It
is the Aether within which Zeus runs
invisibly, and the Akasa through which
Brahm sings his eternal utterance of joy.
The mantle of Mananan, the Aether, the
Akasa, were all associated with Sound as
a creative power, for to the mystic imagination of the past the world was upsung into
being ; and what other thought inspired the
apostle who wrote, " In the beginning was
the Word " ?

Out of the Divine Darkness Mananan has arisen, a brooding twilight before dawn, in which the cloud images of the gods are thronging. But there is still in Lir an immense deep of being, an emotional life too vast, too spiritual, too remote to speak of, for the words we use to-day cannot tell its story. It is the love yet unbreathed, and yet not love, but rather a hidden unutterable tenderness, or joy, or the potency of these, which awakens as the image of the divine imagination is reflected in the being of the Mother, and then it rushes forth to embrace it. The Fountain beneath the Hazel has broken. Creation is astir. The Many are proceeding from the One. An energy or love or eternal desire has gone forth which seeks through a myriad forms of illusion for the infinite being it has left. It is Angus the Young, an eternal joy becoming love, a love changing into desire, and leading on to earthly passion and forgetfulness of its own divinity. The eternal joy becomes love when it has first merged itself in form and images of a divine beauty dance before it and lure it afar. This is the first manifested world, the Tirnanoge or World of Immortal Youth.

The love is changed into desire as it is drawn deeper into nature, and this desire builds up the Mid-world or World of the Waters. And, lastly, as it lays hold of the earthly symbol of its desire it becomes on Earth that passion which is spiritual death. In another sense Angus may be described as the passing into activity of a power latent in Lir, working through the divine imagination, impressing its ideations on nature in its spiritual state, and thereby causing its myriad transformations. It is the fountain in which every energy has its birth, from the power which lays the foundations of the world, down through love and every form of desire to chemical affinity, just as Mananan is the root of all conscious life, from the imperial being of the gods down to the consciousness in the ant or amœba. So is Dana also the basis of every material form from the imperishable body of the immortals to the transitory husk of the gnat. As this divinity emerges from its primordial state of ecstatic tenderness or joy in Lir, its divided rays, incarnate in form, enter upon a threefold life of spiritual love, of desire, and the dark shadow of love ; and these three states have for

themselves three worlds into which they
have transformed the primal nature of
Dana : a World of Immortal Youth : a
Mid-world where everything changes with
desire : and which is called from its fluctua-
tions the World of the Waters : and lastly,
the Earth-world where matter has assumed
that solid form when it appears inanimate
or dead. The force of the fountain which
whirled Sinan away has been spent and
Sinan has met death.

The conception of Angus as an all-
pervading divinity who first connects being
with non-being seems removed by many
aeons of thought from that beautiful golden-
haired youth who plays on the tympan
surrounded by singing birds. But the
golden-haired Angus of the bards has a
relation to the earlier Eros, for in the
mysteries of the Druids all the gods sent
bright witnesses of their boundless being,
who sat enthroned in the palaces of the
Sidhe, and pointed the way to the Land of
Promise to the man who dared become more
than man.

But what in reality is Angus and what is
Dana, and how can they be made real to us?
They will not be gained by much reading of

the legendary tales, for they are already
with us. A child sits on the grass and the
sunlight falls about it. It is lulled by the
soft colour. It grows dreamy, a dreaminess
filled with a vague excitement. It feels a
pleasure, a keen magnetic joy at the touch
of earth : or it lays its head in a silent
tenderness nigh a mother or sister, its mood
impelling it to grow nearer to something it
loves. That tenderness in the big dreamy
heart of childhood is Angus, and the mother-
love it divines is Dana ; and the form which
these all-pervading divinities take in the
heart of the child and the mother, on the
one side desire, on the other a profound
tenderness or pity, are nearest of all the
moods of earth to the first Love and the
Mighty Mother, and through them the
divine may be vaguely understood. If the
desire remains pure, through innocence, or
by reason of wisdom, it becomes in the
grown being a constant preoccupation with
spiritual things, or in words I have quoted
before where it is better said, " The inexpressible yearning of the inner man to go out
into the infinite."

Of Dana, the Hibernian Mother of the
gods, I have already said she is the first

spiritual form of matter, and therefore Beauty. As every being emerges out of her womb clothed with form, she is the Mighty Mother, and as mother of all she is that divine compassion which exists beyond and is the final arbiter of the justice of the gods. Her heart will be in ours when ours forgive.

THE CELTIC IMAGINATION

OTHER names might be used in this Celtic
cosmogenesis and the Dagda stand for Lir,
Boan for Dana, Fintan for Mananan, and
others again might be interchangeable with
these. Even as the generations follow one
another in time, each looking upon the same
unchanging nature as the ancestors but naming
it by other names, so in antiquity races were
invaded by others who came with a cosmogony
the same in all essentials, but for differences
of language and name, as that of the people
invaded. After centuries there comes a
blending of cultures and a subsidence into
legend, bringing about a bewildering mosaic
of mythology. The unity of primeval vision
is broken up in the prism of literature.
Deities grow in number in the popular
imagination and coexist there, who in truth,
if their spiritual ancestry was known, were
but varying names for one divine being.

There are several mythologies in Irish legend
the figures of which are made contemporary
with each other by the later poets, and while
it might be of interest to scholars to dis-
entangle these and relate each deity to its
proper cycle, only the vision of the universe
which underlay them all is of real importance.
That spiritual Overworld our Gaelic ancestors
beheld was in essentials the same as the Overworld revealed in the sacred books ; and in
the wonder tales of the Gael we find a great
secular corroboration of sacred literature and
of half-sacred philosophy such as Plato utters
through the lips of Socrates. Earth, Mid-
world, Heaven-world and the great deep of
deity they knew as they are expounded in the
Upanishads. We can discern the same vision
in the Apostle whose beginning of things was
in the fulness of being out of which arose the
Christos or divine imagination, in which, as
it went forth on its cyclic labours, life or the
Holy Breath was born, or became in it, and
these again shine and work in the darkness
of earth. And when St. Paul speaks of a
third heaven we divine he had risen to the
world of the Christos and was there initiated
into mysteries of which it was not lawful to
speak. In the sacred books there is a pro-

founder life than there is in secular literature
where there is vision indeed, but in the sacred
books there is the being. The mind in
retrospect, meditation and aspiration needs
guidance ; and this spiritual architecture of
Earth-world, with Mid-world, Heaven-world
and God-world rising above it, made my
own vision so far as it went intelligible to me,
for my disconnected glimpses of supernature
seemed to find a place in that architecture of
the heavens. In earlier pages I described my
first visions of other planes, and the beings
there, how some were shining and how others
were a lordlier folk lit up from within as if a
sun was hidden in the heart ; and in my
retrospect of vision I find all I saw falling
into two categories which I think correspond
to the Mid-world and World of Immortal
Youth of the ancestors. My vision into the
highest of these spheres was rare, and only
once did consciousness for a moment follow
vision and I seemed myself to be in the world
I contemplated. At other times I was like
one who cannot enter the gardens of a palace,
but who gazes distantly through gates on
their beauty, and sees people of a higher order
than himself moving in a world enchanting
to his eyes. I did see in some sphere inter-

penetrated with this beings in an ecstasy of radiance, colour and sound, lovers who seemed enraptured with their happiness, as they tell in old story of lovers on the plains of Moy Mell, and to me they seemed like some who had lived in Earth in ancient days and who now were in the happy world. And I saw, without being able to explain to myself their relation to that exalted humanity, beings such as the ancient poets described, a divine folk who I think never were human but were those spoken of as the Sidhe. I did not see enough to enable me to speak with any certainty about their life, and I do not know that it would serve any useful purpose to detail visions which remain bewildering to myself. Into the lowest of these two spheres I saw with more frequency, but was able to understand but little of what I saw. I will tell one or two visions out of many. I was drawn to meditate beside a deep pool amid woods. It was a place charged with psychic life, and was regarded with some awe by the people who lived near. As I gazed into the dark waters consciousness seemed to sink beneath them and I found myself in another world. It was more luminous than this, and I found one there who seemed like an elemental king. He was seated on a throne, and I saw that a lustrous air rose up as from a fountain beneath the seat and his breathing of it gave him power. The figure was of a brilliant blue and gold opalescence, and the breast, as with many of the higher beings, was shining, and a golden light seemed to pervade the whole body and to shine through its silvery blueness. The tribe he ruled were smaller than himself, and these I saw descending on the right of the throne, their shining dimmed to a kind of greyness, and each one as it came before the throne bent forward and pressed its lips upon the heart of the king, and in an instant at the touch it became flushed with life and it shot up plumed and radiant, and there was a continuous descent on one side of grey elementals and on the other side a continuous ascent of radiant figures, and I know not what it meant. And at another time I saw one of these lesser beings flying as a messenger out of the heart of one greater, and I saw a return to the heart and the vanishing of the lesser in the greater, and I know not what it meant. And at another time I was astonished, for I saw rising out of deep water seven shining and silvery figures, and three on one side and three on another side and one beneath, they held uplifted hands on the hilt of a gigantic sword of quivering flame, and they waved that mighty sword in air and sank again beneath the waters. And after that seven others rose up and they held a great spear, and it they pointed skywards and sank below ; and after that arose two carrying a cauldron, and, when they had vanished, one solitary figure arose and it held in its hands a great and glittering stone ; and why these beautiful beings should bring forth the four precious symbols of the Tuatha de Danaan I do not know, for that Mid-world, as Usheen travelling to Tirnanoge saw, is full of strange and beautiful forms appearing and vanishing ever about the mystic adventurer, and there are to be seen many beings such as the bards told of : beings riding like Lir or Mananan upon winged steeds, or surrounded like Angus Oge with many-coloured birds, and why these images of beauty and mystery should be there I do not know, but they entered into the imagination of poets in the past and have entered into the imagination of others who are still living. I can only surmise that they were given the names of Mananan, Angus, Dana or Lir because they were mouthpieces of the bodiless deities and perhaps sitting on high thrones represented these at the Druidic mysteries, and when the mortal came to be made immortal they spoke to him each out of their peculiar wisdom. In myself as in others I know they awakened ecstasy. To one who lay on the mound which is called the Brugh on the Boyne a form like that the bards speak of Angus appeared, and it cried: "Can you not see me? Can you not hear me? I come from the Land of Immortal Youth." And I, though I could not be certain of speech, found the wild words flying up to my brain interpreting my own vision of the god, and it seemed to be crying to me : "Oh, see our sun is dawning for us, ever dawning, with ever youthful and triumphant voices. Your sun is but a smoky shadow : ours the ruddy and eternal glow. Your fire is far away, but ours within our hearts is ever living and through wood and wave is ever dawning on adoring eyes. My birds from purple fiery plumage shed the light of lights. Their kisses wake the love that never dies and leads through death to me. My love shall be in thine when love is sacrifice." I do not believe that either to myself or my friend were such words spoken, but the whole being

is lifted up in vision and overmastered, and
the words that came flying upward in consciousness perhaps represent our sudden harmony with a life which is beyond ourselves,
we in our words interpreting the life of the
spirit.   Some interpret the spirit with sadness
and some with joy, but in this country I think
it will always cry out its wild and wondrous
story of immortal youth and will lead its
votaries to a heaven where they will be
drunken with beauty.   What is all this?
Poetry or fantasy?   It has visited thousands
in all ages and lands, and from such visions
have come all that is most beautiful in poetry
or art.   These forms inhabited Shelley's
luminous cloudland, and they were the models
in the Pheidian heart, and they have been
with artist, poet and musician since the
beginning of the world, and they will be with
us until we grow into their beauty and learn
from them how to fulfil human destiny,
accomplishing our labour which is to make
this world into the likeness of the Kingdom
of Light.

EARTH

I THINK of earth as the floor of a cathedral where altar and Presence are everywhere. This reverence came to me as a boy listening to the voice of birds one coloured evening in summer, when suddenly birds and trees and grass and tinted air and myself seemed but one mood or companionship, and I felt a certitude that the same spirit was in all. A little breaking of the barriers and being would mingle with being. Whitman writes of the earth that it is rude and incomprehensible at first. "But I swear to you," he cries, "that there are divine things well hidden." Yet they are not so concealed that the lover may not discover them, and to the lover nature reveals herself like a shy maiden who is slowly drawn to one who adores her at a distance, and who is first acknowledged by a lifting of the veil, a long-remembered glance, a glimmering smile, and at last comes speech

and the mingling of life with life. So the
lover of Earth obtains his reward, and little
by little the veil is lifted of an inexhaustible
beauty and majesty. It may be he will be
tranced in some spiritual communion, or will
find his being overflowing into the being of
the elements, or become aware that they are
breathing their life into his own. Or Earth
may become on an instant all faery to him,
and earth and air resound with the music of
its invisible people. Or the trees and rocks
may waver before his eyes and become
transparent, revealing what creatures were
hidden from him by the curtain, and he will
know as the ancients did of dryad and hama-
dryad, of genii of wood and mountain. Or
earth may suddenly blaze about him with
supernatural light in some lonely spot amid
the hills, and he will find he stands as the
prophet in a place that is holy ground, and
he may breathe the intoxicating exhalations
as did the sibyls of old. Or his love may
hurry him away in dream to share in deeper
mysteries, and he may see the palace chambers
of nature where the wise ones dwell in secret,
looking out over the nations, breathing power
into this man's heart or that man's brain,
on any who appear to their vision to wear

the colour of truth. So gradually the earth
lover realises the golden world is all about
him in imperishable beauty, and he may pass
from the vision to the profounder beauty of
being, and know an eternal love is within
and around him, pressing upon him and sus-
taining with infinite tenderness his body, his
soul and his spirit.

I have obscured the vision of that being
by dilating too much on what was curious,
but I desired to draw others to this meditation,
if by reasoning it were possible to free the
intellect from its own fetters, so that the
imagination might go forth, as Blake says,
"in uncurbed glory." So I stayed the vision
which might have been art, or the ecstasy
which might have been poetry, and asked of
them rather to lead me back to the ancestral
fountain from which they issued. I think
by this meditation we can renew for ourselves
the magic and beauty of Earth, and understand
the meaning of things in the sacred books
which had grown dim. We have so passed
away from vital contact with divine powers
that they have become for most names for
the veriest abstractions, and those who read
do not know that the Mighty Mother is that
Earth on which they tread and whose holy

substance they call common clay ; or that the
Paraclete is the strength of our being, the
power which binds atom to atom and Earth
to Heaven : or that the Christos is the
Magician of the Beautiful and that it is not
only the Architect of the God-world but is
that in us which sees beauty, creates beauty,
and it is verily wisdom in us and is our
deepest self ; or that the Father is the fountain
of substance and power and wisdom, and that
we could not lift an eyelash but that we have
our being in Him. When we turn from
books to living nature we begin to understand
the ancient wisdom, and it is no longer an
abstraction, for the Great Spirit whose home
is in the vast becomes for us a moving
glamour in the heavens, a dropping tenderness
at twilight, a visionary light in the hills, a
voice in the heart, the Earth underfoot becomes sacred, and the air we breathe is like
wine poured out for us by some heavenly
cupbearer.

As we grow intimate with earth we realise
what sweet and august things await humanity
when it goes back to that forgotten mother.
Who would be ambitious, who would wish
to fling a name like Caesar's in the air, if he
saw what thrones and majesties awaited the

heavenly adventurer? Who would hate if
he could see beneath the husk of the body
the spirit which is obscured and imprisoned
there, and how it was brother to his own
spirit and all were children of the King?
Who would weary of nature or think it a
solitude once the veil had been lifted for him,
once he had seen that great glory? Would
they not long all of them for the coming of
that divine hour in the twilights of time,
when out of rock, mountain, water, tree, bird,
beast or man the seraph spirits of all that live
shall emerge realising their kinship, and all
together, fierce things made gentle, and timid
things made bold, and small made great, shall
return to the Father Being and be made one
in Its infinitudes.

When we attain this vision nature will
melt magically before our eyes, and powers
that seem dreadful, things that seemed
abhorrent in her, will reveal themselves as
brothers and allies. Until then she is
unmoved by our conflicts and will carry on
her ceaseless labours.

> No sign is made while empires pass.
> The flowers and stars are still His care,
> The constellations hid in grass,
> The golden miracles in air.

Life in an instant will be rent
When death is glittering, blind and wild,
The Heavenly Brooding is intent
To that last instant on Its child.

It breathes the glow in brain and heart.
Life is made magical.   Until
Body and spirit are apart
The Everlasting works Its will.

In that wild orchid that your feet
In their next falling shall destroy,
Minute and passionate and sweet,
The Mighty Master holds His joy.

Though the crushed jewels droop and fade
The Artist's labours will not cease,
And from the ruins shall be made
Some yet more lovely masterpiece.